# Ward Walks to Wet Your Whistle

by
Roger Seedhouse

Meridian Books

Published 2003 by Meridian Books

© Roger Seedhouse 2003

ISBN 1-869922-48-4

A catalogue record for this book is available from the British Library.

Meridian Books
40 Hadzor Road, Oldbury, West Midlands B68 9LA

Printed in Great Britain by Juma, Sheffield

# Contents

# Introduction

Warwickshire, the centre of England and a county of great contrasts. Historic, bustling towns interspersed with pretty, quiet villages – some of which almost convey the impression that they are still waiting to be discovered. For many people, of course, they are and I hope this book will help in some small way to bring into focus the rich variety of landscape which the county stands justly proud of.

It is hard to imagine that the north of the county, so close as it is to the huge urban sprawls of Birmingham and Coventry (not to mention motorways) can contain such beauty. Just a short detour from the concrete jungle will reveal a land of lakes and country parks which are a delight to behold. Moving south, the area around the celebrated centres of Warwick and Stratford-upon-Avon give way to a more rolling topography which progressively merges into the Northern Cotswolds with its villages of honey-hued stone – the epitome of England at its finest So, please go out and sample all that it has to offer.

## Perceptions

When it comes to walking, attitudes vary enormously. Some would be filled with dread at the prospect of having to walk half a mile; others would regard a twenty mile trek as little more than a stroll. This publication is aimed at what is probably the vast majority of us who fall somewhere between these two extremes.

## Pleasures

You've heard it before but I'll say it again – walking is good for you! It is an inexpensive way to get exercise and allows you to see at close hand the wonderful countryside with which this island is blessed. It is amazing how much hidden beauty there is even on your own doorstep – go out and enjoy it!

## Pubs

A pub is not essential for a good walk but the two combine admirably together. Many walkers appreciate a watering hole *en route* or at the end of a walk – not extremely 'posh' pubs serving expensive meals (walkers don't tend to be popular in such places) but simple country locals where they can take a break and sample the unique character which some of them possess. However, there is no point in having a great pub and an indifferent walk, or vice versa, and in striking a balance it is inevitable that there will be a mix of pub types, although I have endeavoured to confine the choice to those where the walker will feel at ease. It is an unfortunate symptom of modern times that many country pubs are struggling to survive and some find it to be not worthwhile opening during weekday lunch-times. Notes on individual opening times are given in the Factfiles, though I am unable to guarantee that there have not been any changes since going to press.

## Points to consider

1. Wear sensible gear. A good pair of boots is essential; so are waterproofs and warm clothing in less clement weather or when undertaking wild hill walks.

2. If you can, take a map of the area. Landranger (1:50,000) is the most commonly used but Explorer (1:25,000) with much more detail is better. I am not suggesting this because you are likely to get lost but merely as a prudent precaution just in case you do stray off the route or if, perhaps because of deteriorating weather, you want to cut short the walk. A compass is also a valuable item for the same reasons.

3. Some paths, particularly those less well used, can get overgrown in summer. A walking stick can make life a lot easier in such situations and, sometimes, a pair of secateurs. A small first aid kit should also be carried in the event of a close encounter with a bramble or other mishap.

4. The countryside is constantly changing. Seasonal changes can make things which appear obvious or easy to recognise in summer less so in winter and vice versa. Be wary also of physical changes. The position or type of gate/fence/stile may be altered, field boundaries are changed or even removed altogether, tracks can be diverted (officially or otherwise), etc.

5. Without wishing to state the obvious, give consideration to the choice of time to do a particular walk. Not the time of day necessarily, although you will need to allow adequate time to complete the main walks, but the time of year. You may wish to avoid those walks covering intensively farmed areas during, say, June – August when paths over cropped fields can be a problem. Even though landowners are under a legal obligation to maintain paths after planting, some of them don't. Similarly, I would not advise walking over very hilly country on an iffy winter's day.

6. A Right of Way is precisely what it says – you have the right to walk along it at all times unimpeded. Fortunately, most County Councils pursue a continuing programme of clearing and waymarking paths, but this is a huge task and many remain obscure. Likewise, most landowners adopt an enlightened attitude towards walkers but occasionally obstructions will be encountered, paths will have been obliterated or diverted or not reinstated after planting has taken place. Try not to be daunted by such things and remember that you have a legal right to pass. Needless to say, common sense should come to the fore in such situations; for example, it may be necessary to take a path around the edge of a cropped field rather than across it or follow an unofficial diversion rather than stick to the line on the map. Any serious obstructions should, however, be reported to Warwickshire Council's Rights of Way department – the address is given at the end of this introduction.

7. Some animals can create consternation for the walker. Farm dogs are frequently encountered but mostly make a lot of noise rather than cause any physical injury. Again, a walking stick is useful just to be on the safe side. A field of frisky young bullocks is best avoided. Even though they are merely curious or think you have come to feed them, I prefer to skirt around them where possible. Sheep are no problem!

8. Not many landlords like muddy boots trampling over their floors. Try to be considerate and, if you cannot clean them off, take them off and leave outside or in a lobby.

9. Warwickshire is reasonably well served by public transport so if you prefer to travel this way you can find bus and train by consulting the services listed at the end of this section.

10. Last, but not least, REMEMBER THE COUNTRY CODE!

| |
|---|
| Enjoy the country and respect its life and work.<br>Guard against all risk of fire.<br>Keep dogs under close control.<br>Keep to public footpaths across farmland.<br>Use gates and stiles to cross field boundaries.<br>Leave all livestock, machinery and crops alone.<br>Take your litter home.Help to keep all water clean.<br>Protect wildlife, plants and trees.<br>Make no unnecessary noise.<br>Fasten all gates. |

# The Walks

The shorter walks are all contained within the route of the main walks and those paths applicable to short routes only are denoted by dots on the sketch maps.

Main walks are designed so that the pub break is roughly at the halfway point; shorter routes start and finish at the pub. Individual circumstances may dictate a change of start point to fit in with public transport or pub opening times.

Grid references (GR) for the starting points are given in the Factfiles. If you are unfamiliar with the use of these you will find details on Ordnance Survey Landranger maps.

Reference points on the maps are shown in the text thus:

Other than at busy times, most landlords will not object to you leaving a car on their car park if you are going to patronise the pub when you return, but if in any doubt please ask permission.

Problems with paths should be reported to
Warwickshire County Council
The Countryside Access Team
Unit 11
Montague Road
Warwick
CV34 5LW
Or e-mail: paths@warwickshire.gov.uk.

Public transport information can be obtained from Traveline on 0870 608 2608; through its website www.traveline.org.uk; and through the Warwickshire website: www.warwickshire.gov.uk

GOOD WALKING!

# The Asterisk

Asterisks will be found in various places in the texts of the walks, placed after one of the features in respect of which information is provided below. This has been done to avoid repetition and save space!

## Centenary Way

The County Council's 100 mile Long Distance Footpath runs from the north to the south of the county linking all the Country Parks and three historic towns to make a grand tour of Warwickshire. From Kingsbury Water Park it runs east to visit Hartshill Hayes near Nuneaton, then south via paths, tracks and canal towpaths to Coombe Abbey near Coventry. Passing south of the city and close to the River Avon, the walk runs through the village of Stoneleigh, site of the Royal Agricultural Show, Kenilworth with its castle, and Warwick. Then comes a delightful stroll through public parks beside the rivers Avon and Leam to the east of Leamington Spa. Returning to the canals, the Way heads south across open country to cross the sheep cropped Burton Dassett Hills and joins the ridge of Edge Hill. After Shipston-on-Stour and Ilmington the walk ends at Upper Quinton on the Gloucestershire border. At both ends it meets the Heart of England Way.

## The Heart of England Way

The Heart of England Way runs 100 miles through the green heart of England, linking Staffordshire with the Cotswolds. Crossing Cannock Chase, it leaves the Iron Age fort of Castle Ring and falls gently to Lichfield. South and then east into the Tame Valley at Drayton Bassett, it joins the Birmingham and Fazeley Canal, passes through Kingsbury Water Park and on to Shustoke.

For the next 30 miles the landscape is typically 'Arden' – hilly, green and well wooded. Passing Meriden, Centre of England, the Way visits pretty English Villages such as Berkswell, the moated Baddesley Clinton Hall and a procession of rural churches. Crossing the Grand Union and Stratford Canals it makes for Henley-in-Arden then Alcester.

After a climb past Oversley Castle the Way falls into the valley of the River Arrow at Wixford and a flat, willowy landscape. The Arrow joins the Avon at Bidford and the Way crosses the fertile 'fruit and veg' county of Vale of Evesham to Meon Hill and the Cotswolds.

After the lovely village of Chipping Campden the walk heads south through a landscape of long shouldered hills and deep woody valleys, with the stones, the houses and the soil in honey and grey. The Way passes Batsford Arboretum and through the parkland of the extravagant oriental palace of Sezincote towards Swell and Lower Slaughter. There is no more climbing but a steady, slow fall through a land of clear, fast, weed trailing brooks, weirs, tiny stone clapper bridges and low, green meadows to Bourton-on-the-Water.

## Birmingham and Fazeley Canal

The Canal was opened in 1789 and is relatively minute, running for a total length of only 15 miles between the centre of Birmingham to Fazeley Junction near Lichfield. It has 38 locks on it though, most of which are contained in two flights of 13 and 11 in Birmingham.

# Oxford Canal

The 77 mile **Oxford Canal Walk** follows the meandering towpaths of the Oxford Canal as it passes through the counties of Oxfordshire, Warwickshire and Northamptonshire. Providing a continuous route between Oxford and Coventry, the walk links beautiful rural villages and bustling urban centres.

# Grand Union Canal

The Grand Union Canal leaves the River Thames at Brentford and climbs over 50 locks up into the Chiltern hills. It descends then climbs again to a new summit in Birmingham, 137 miles and 166 locks later. Boatmen used to claim to do it in five days but allow well over a week if you want to get any sleep! The Leicester section branches north at Braunston and climbs a little less steeply before falling to join the River Soar which flows into the River Trent. It has 59 locks and is 66 miles long.

# The Monarch's Way

A long distance path tracking the flight of Charles II after his defeat at the Battle of Worcester in 1651 and his subsequent escape to France. He first travelled north, then south through the Cotswolds and the Mendips, and finally along the South Downs to Shoreham where he finally eluded his pursuers. The walk using footpaths and bridleways closely follows Charles's route and includes many historic sites and buildings.

# Stratford-upon-Avon Canal

The Stratford-Upon-Avon Canal runs for just 25 miles from the Birmingham suburbs to the River Avon in Stratford-upon-Avon. There are 54 locks so two days are needed. Although the canal is fairly short it goes through some enchanting countryside in the very Heart of England, cutting through the Forest of Arden with its ancient oaks, an area rich in Shakespearian links.

Leaving the Birmingham suburbs the canal falls gently across quiet rolling countryside and watermeadows to the Avon, passing through nothing other than small villages until it reaches Stratford. The delightfully named neighbouring Warwickshire villages of Preston Bagot, Wootton Wawen and Wilmcote are all attractive with old houses, churches, inns and Halls or Manors. The cottage of Mary Arden, Shakespeare's mother, is at Wilmcote and the other two have Norman or Saxon churches. Lapworth is an interesting canal junction where a short spur connects to the Grand Union Canal which runs close by. The final descent through the Stratford suburbs is uninspiring until you pass under a low bridge to emerge amongst hordes of visitors in Stratford Basin, alongside the River Avon and right outside the Shakespeare Memorial Theatre.

# Arden Way

The Arden Way is a 26-mile circular walk in the Forest of Arden area of Warwickshire in attractive countryside near to Stratford-upon-Avon and the home of Shakespeare. The Way takes the walker through some of the finest landscape in the county using field paths, tracks, lanes and woodland paths as it meanders through typically rolling Warwickshire countryside.

In Shakespeare's day, the Forest of Arden was thickly wooded and covered some 200 square miles to the north and west of the river Avon but it was largely cut down during the Industrial Revolution when the trees were used as fuel for the iron works of the Midlands. Today, the forest comprises scattered woodland

and there is a tree planting programme taking place with the intention of restoring parts of the forest to its former glory.

The Arden Way starts in the very heart of the Forest of Arden at the historic market town of Henley-in-Arden. Henley-in-Arden is an attractive medieval town with many half-timbered fifteenth, sixteenth and seventeenth century buildings adorned with floral arrangements in summer ready for the Britain in Bloom competition and for local events often led by its colourful Court Leet. Two old inns – the White Swan (sixteenth century) and the Blue Bell (seventeenth century) are particular attractions. There is a fifteenth century Guildhall and nearby are the earthwork remains of Beaudesert Castle.

The Way takes the walker through the village of Ullenhall before proceeding over undulating pastureland to pass in front of the magnificent Coughton Court (NT). The Court has been the home of the Throckmorton family since the fifteenth century and is famous for its connection with the Gunpowder Plot in 1605.

As the route nears Roman Alcester it joins the nationally known Heart of England Way which leads the walker into the olde-worlde High Street of Roman Alcester where one can admire many timber-fronted houses with old windows, several old coaching inns and a fine seventeenth century timber-topped town hall – you may be lucky enough to be in town when the Town Crier's competition is in full swing. In 1996, Alcester won the 'National Britain in Bloom' competition and the town is a floral picture during the summer months.

Approximately a mile and a half SW of Alcester is Ragley Hall (AD1680), the home of the Marquis of Hertford – the building has a superb interior and a fine park, landscaped by Capability Brown.

From Alcester the Way continues past some magnificent thatched houses in Oversley Green and after passing along the edge of bluebell woods, meanders through several attractive period hamlets before arriving at Aston Cantlow where the King's Arms Inn always offers a warm welcome.

The Arden Way rejoins the Heart of England Way near Shelfield Green and continues over beautiful undulating Warwickshire countryside passing through clumps of the original Arden Forest to arrive back at Henley-in-Arden. The walk ends after passing through the railway station to arrive in the attractive High Street.

## Ridge Fields

A noticeable feature that you will sometimes meet is ridge and furrow surface undulations. Because the ground has been relatively undisturbed over the centuries, the remains of this medieval open field system of farming can still clearly be seen. The fields were cultivated in strips, each villager having a certain number of strips depending upon his trade and position in society. The strips were ploughed as separate units which built them up into ridges, the furrows acting as boundaries with the neighbouring strips.

The normal length of a strip was one furlong (220 yards), which was deemed to be the distance that an ox could be expected to pull a plough without a rest. The width was one perch (5.5 yards) and the area was known as a rod, or a quarter of an acre.

# About the author

Roger Seedhouse is a Chartered Surveyor and a partner in a firm of property consultants in the West Midlands. Much of his time is spent surveying industrial property in the less picturesque parts of the West Midlands, so walking in the countryside provides an excellent contrast to this. He has two 'grown-up' daughters and spends much of his spare time walking and developing his website www.bestwalks.com.

# Acknowledgments

I am indebted to Patricia Wootton for the help and assistance she has given me in the preparation of this book.

*The Cottage of Content, Barton (Walk 13)*

---

## Publishers' Note

Every care has been taken in the preparation of this book. All the walks have been independently checked and are believed to be correct at the time of publication. However, neither the author nor the publishers can accept responsibility for any errors or omissions or for any loss, damage, injury or inconvenience resulting from the use of the book.

Please remember that the countryside is continually changing: hedges and fences may be removed or re-sited; landmarks may disappear; footpaths may be re-routed or be ploughed over and not reinstated (as the law requires); concessionary paths may be closed. The publishers would be very pleased to have details of any such changes that are observed by readers.

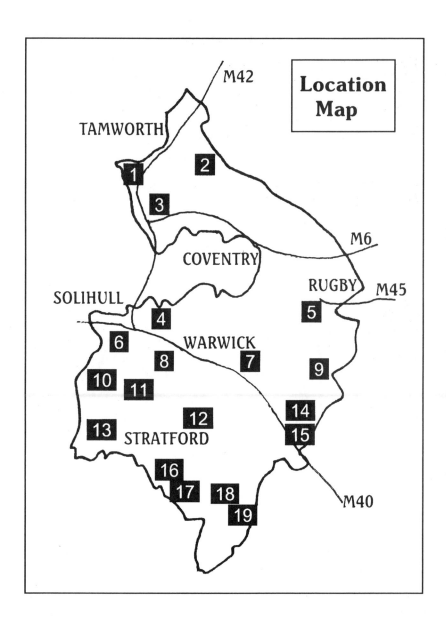

Location Map

TAMWORTH

M42

COVENTRY

M6

SOLIHULL

RUGBY    M45

WARWICK

STRATFORD

M40

# Kingsbury Water Park

## Fact*file*

**Maps:** Explorer 232; Landranger 139
**Distances:** Main walk 7 miles: shorter walk 4.75 miles
**Main Start:** The Broomey Croft car park at Kingsbury Water Park, Bodymoor Heath, three miles north of Junction 9 M42, just off the A4091. Follow the sign left immediately after crossing the humpbacked bridge over the Birmingham and Fazeley Canal – do not cross the M42 and go in the main entrance unless you want to pay a higher car parking charge. The cost per car is £1.10 but don't let that put you off. GR 204969.
**Short Start:** The Dog and Doublet, a canal side pub at Bodymoor Heath – see above for location. GR198962. Alternatively, you could start from the Broomey Croft car park as it is *en route*.
**Terrain:** Very easy going on well used paths through a very watery landscape and particularly interesting if you are a bird watcher. A wonderful walk at any time of year combining a large part of the Water Park, a section of the Birmingham and Fazeley Canal and the stately Middleton Hall, which is in process of restoration. Absolutely no climbs at all. It should be noted that the Water Park can get busy at popular times.

## The Pub

**The Dog and Doublet, Bodymoor Heath:** A three-storey, probably Georgian, property situated right on the canalside with a wonderful terrace with seating right alongside where you can relax on a nice day and simply watch the narrowboats negotiating the lock. That is if you can get a seat – if not there is a pleasant grassed beer garden on the other side where BBQ's are going at busy times. All in all a super pub with a convivial atmosphere, serving Worthington, Bass, Murphys, Highgate Dark Mild, Caffreys, Stella Artois, Carling, Blackthorne Cider plus wine on draught. Internally the pub is totally unspoilt with beamed ceilings, open fireplaces and brass plaques everywhere with little mottos like 'No bloody swearing' and 'Hands off the barmaid!' Open Mon-Fri 11.30-2.30 and 6-11; Sat all day; Sun 12-3 and 6-10.30. Tel: 01827 872374

From the car park walk across the grassed area and turn left onto the path around Broomey Croft Pool facing you. At a junction bear right along the adjacent side of it. Keep going past Canal Pool which, as the name implies, brings you alongside the Birmingham and Fazeley Canal* and you are shortly obliged to drop down onto the canal towpath. Walk along the towpath for about a mile until arriving at Fisher's Mill Bridge. Before getting there you will pass under two metal bridges, both of which are utilised in connection with quarrying activity in the area. If you do this walk during the week you will see and hear lots of this activity which might, I suppose, be a little off-putting; however, I found it quite fascinating and a stark contrast to the usual rural sights and sounds. The first of these two bridges carries quarry traffic but the second is a materials conveyor belt which runs for, maybe, a mile and a half between the gravel pit to the north of the Water Park and the main depot at Coneybury (which you will skirt round later). As you reach Fisher's Mill Bridge you can see and hear the conveyor belt rumbling along in front of you. You can also see the Lichfield Transmitter to the north and the Sutton Coldfield Transmitter to the west.

At the bridge leave by going up the embankment, turn left over the bridge and then keep left at a junction of paths on a rough track. For a short while you are 'doubling back' on the opposite side of the canal and have to work your way across a little bridge over a stream which actually passes under the canal and links up with the River Tame nearby. Continue on the path which emerges

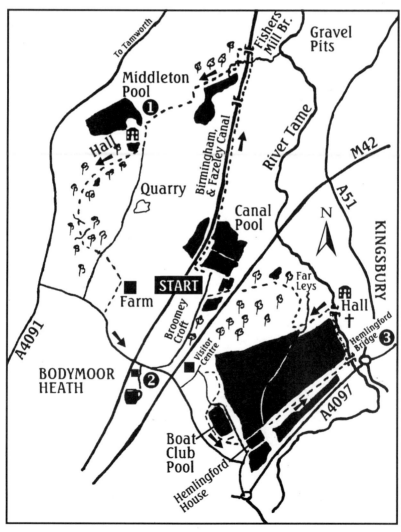

# Kingsbury Water Park

*Kingsbury Water Park*

alongside another lake heading towards a farm. Again, you can see the conveyor belt on the other side. Beyond the lake continue on a grass track before turning left at a waymark towards the farm then right on reaching it. You shortly go across a quarry track and continue until reaching a junction with Middleton Hall directly in front. Here we need to go left unless the Hall is open and you wish to visit it or the craft workshop nearby. You could also walk a little further around to the right to view the attractive Middleton Pool. **❶**

*Middleton Hall is a Grade II listed building which dates back to 1300 and stands in a pleasant park of about 40 acres. Visited by Queen Elizabeth I, it was the house of two great seventeenth century naturalists, Francis Willoughby and John Ray and is a mixture of architectural styles, the most spectacular being the Georgian West Wing. An earlier Francis Willoughby was an unfortunate man, having got into great debt and later poisoned by his wife. A gruesome discovery was made in the mid nineteenth century when it was decided to do away with the moat – the skeleton of a horse and rider in armour. Apparently a courier from the Royalist Army at the battle of Edge Hill in 1642 lost his bearings in dense fog and tripped over the parapet into the moat. The Hall is no longer lived in but is used as a conference and event facility. The Tudor wing promises to be an interesting feature once restoration has been completed by the Middleton Hall Trust. The property is open on Sundays and Bank Holidays from April to September, 2-5pm. Admission £2.00 or £3.00 on Bank Holidays. Refreshments available. The craft centre is also housed in a Tudor building and is open Wed-Sun, 11am-5pm. Tel: 01827 283095*

Having turned left in front of the hall continue round onto a broad shaled track past the rear of the Hall and towards the main quarry depot. Look carefully for a waymarked permissive route on your right which will take you around the quarry on a much more pleasant route, although you can continue on the definitive route through the quarry site if you wish. I would, however, advise you to go with the waymark into Lakeside Wood, shortly keeping right at a fork along a grassy track and stay with it as it loops left into a belt of trees. On reaching a pool another waymark directs you left along the edge of a field but, after about 100 yards, you are brought back into the tree belt and cross a footbridge before continuing ahead through the trees. You cross another couple of footbridges before the path swings left and eventually brings you out via a stile onto a tarmac lane. You have now successfully by-passed the quarry.

Cross the lane almost directly over another stile into a field which you walk over towards the left most and largest oak in a sparse line on the far boundary. Ahead you can see the bulk of Kingsbury Oil Terminal, unfortunately. When you get there (not the oil terminal) go through into the next field and turn right along the right edge of it bordering a ditch. Exit via a gate and turn left on a lane and stay on it until reaching a humpback bridge over the Birmingham and Fazeley canal. Cross it carefully and turn left then left again under the bridge and down the towpath for a short distance to a lock, on the far side of which is the Dog and Doublet. **2**

*The Dog and Doublet*

It almost required a superior force to get me motivated to leave here but, in the end, a sharp kick from my partner was enough. On leaving, reverse your steps back under the bridge and emerge to turn left along the lane towards the Broomey Croft entrance to Kingsbury Water Park. If you want to cut short the walk here simply turn into the entrance and follow the driveway back to the car park – probably the same driveway you drove along earlier. Those opting for the extension walk should continue along the lane, over the M42 (lovely!) and turn left at the main entrance to the Water Park.

*Kingsbury Water Park. Formed from worked out gravel pits it comprises thirteen landscaped lakes plus numerous pools in 620 acres managed by Warwickshire County Council and caters for a diverse range of leisure activities, including walking (of course), bird watching, fishing, cycling and sailing. The visitor centre is very informative and also contains a shop and café/restaurant. The park is open all year round but opening and closing times get progressively later and earlier towards and during the winter months. Tel: 01827 872660.*

# Kingsbury Water Park

Go past the visitor centre and turn right at the 'mini' island then shortly branch off left to reach what is the largest of the lakes (Bodymoor Heath Water) and bear right onto the path running alongside it. On reaching a junction with tarmac again cross it diagonally to proceed along the right side of the model boat club pool. As you will probably have noticed we are on the Centenary Way* here which links all of the County's Country Parks. Unless you want to divert in order to look at something particular keep on the main path until reaching another junction with tarmac. Here go right to resume the walk along the adjacent edge of the large lake and with a much smaller one to your right behind Hemlingford House. The driveway swings left and you keep going until arriving at Hemlingford Bridge across the River Tame. ❸

You don't actually cross the bridge but turn left immediately in front of it across a grassy patch which takes you onto a path between the lake and the river. The town of Kingsbury is now to your right and you can see the church ahead. When you get there you will see also the ruins of the once proud Hall. The town has a long history going back to Saxon times (the Saxon name for Kingsbury is 'Chinesburie' meaning a royal fortified site, which is given credence by its position on a bluff above the River Tame – a perfect place for fortification) and was held by Earl Leofric and his wife, the Countess of Godiva. The Hall was built by Thomas Bracebridge the Younger and eventually passed to the Peel family from Drayton Manor and was occupied by four successive Sir Robert Peels before falling into ruin. You can cross the bridge to look at the church if you wish but it is normally kept locked. A list of key-holders is posted in the porch. There is no access to the Hall. If you decide not to go across get on to the raised walkway cutting back towards the lake. Why is the walkway raised? Answers on a postcard to… er, no perhaps not on second thoughts!

At the end the walkway crosses a brook and you veer round to the right along a path going away from the lake. Ignore the first waymark on the right immediately after the brook crossing but, at the second, after only another 50 yards or so turn off right along a narrow grassy track through trees. After a few yards stay ahead at crosstracks and continue until arrival at a junction with a partly surfaced driveway where you turn left onto it. Keep immediately right at a fork along the main track which is again a section of the Centenary Way* and you will come to Far Leys car park. Be careful over direction now. Keep to the right of the car park and past the toilets – stopping there if need must – then as the driveway loops left turn off right by a sign down a gravel path then almost straight away branch off left down another path. If you come to a children's play area you have gone too far.

You very shortly pass to the left of an attractive pool and keep going through a not so attractive tunnel under the M42 and, a short distance after emerging, bear right at a waymark following the signs to Broomey Croft Car Park. Keep going until you get there.

## Shorter Walks

The main walk is basically split into two sections and either could effectively become a shorter walk. In both cases I would suggest that you start/finish at the Dog and Doublet although you could use the Broomey Croft car park. See text after point (2) for directions between the pub and the car park.

# Hartshill and Bentley

## Fact*file*

**Maps:** Explorer 232; Landranger 140

**Distances:** Main walk 7 miles; shorter walk 3.25 miles

**Main Start:** The Hartshill Hayes Country Park main car park, Hartshill, which is located roughly halfway between Nuneaton and Atherstone. You need to take a turning to the left off the road out of Hartshill towards the A5 and Atherstone (or right if approaching from the north) and the car park is situated on the right after about two-thirds of a mile. It is fairly well signed. There is a charge of £1.20 towards the upkeep of the park. Open all year round from 9am although closing times vary according to the time of year between 4 and 9pm. GR 316944

**Short Start:** The Horse and Jockey in the small hamlet of Bentley which is on the B4116 about three miles south-west of Atherstone. GR 283957

**Terrain:** A fascinating mix of open space wedged between urban sprawl, beautiful woodland and little tucked away settlements. Some excellent views even though there is always a backdrop of built-up areas. A few gradients but nothing too energetic.

### The Pub:

**The Horse and Jockey, Bentley**
An interesting place which successfully caters for both the 'local' trade and fairly up-market restaurant clients. There are two bars which are quite basic but with a welcoming pubby atmosphere even on a weekday lunchtime. Good for walkers – no danger of messing up the expensive carpet! Serving Bass, John Smiths, Guinness, Fosters, Theakson's Mild, Carling, Stella Artois and Strongbow. There is usually at least one guest beer. You can get bar snacks or eat sumptuously in the adjoining brasserie. Open each day 12-3 and 5.30-10.30. The brasserie is closed on Monday lunchtimes. Tel: 01827 715236

*Incorporating 136 acres of open hilltop and woodland on a ridge overlooking the Anker Valley, Hartshill Hayes Country Park was opened in 1978 by Warwickshire County Council with help from the Countryside Commission. The open hilltop offers panoramic views across four counties and on a clear day it is possible to see the Derbyshire Peaks, Leicestershire's Charnwood Forest and the less picturesque Drakelow Power Station! The excellent view is doubtless one of the reasons why the site was chosen for a fort in the Iron Age. The old earthworks led the Saxons to call the site Ealdbury – meaning an old fortified place, although down the centuries the name has become the present day Oldbury – which still means the same.*

# Hartshill and Bentley

Today the fort's outlines are harder to pick out, although parts of the earth embankments and outer defences can still be recognised despite the heavy overgrowth of bushes and brambles. The Hayes itself is reputed to be a remnant of the old Forest of Arden, although much of it was replanted at the end of the eighteenth century. It is a mixed woodland with examples of trees which have been coppiced – that is their main trunks have been cut and the resultant shoots which spring from the base have been cultivated. In the case of The Hayes, the timber from the coppiced limes was used by Atherstone hat-makers to make the hat blocks on which felt hats were moulded. Oak used to be the dominant tree in the woods but most of these were cropped by the Forestry Commission in 1981, although a major feature at the furthest point is The Clump of Oaks, some 35 mature trees standing on a small hillock which are about 130 years old. The Romans made pottery and glass in the area and the remains of their kilns have been found nearby. They also quarried the hard Cambrian rocks such as quartzite, which are still quarried nearby and used for road making. Near Mancetter in the valley below the park was probably the last battleground of the Celtic queen, Boudicca (Boadicea) who was defeated by the Romans in AD60-61. Also nearby is the site of Oldbury Hall, which was built in the eighteenth century but which was partially destroyed by incendiary bombs during the Second World War and demolished after it became a favourite target for vandals.

From the visitor centre go out to the rear on a path signed St. Lawrence's Wood and Hill Top Meadow viewpoint onto a broad gravel track. You very soon keep left at a fork along the upper path where you are immediately presented with panoramic views over Atherstone and surrounding countryside. Where the gravel ends go straight ahead over a grassed area in front of some benches after which you bear right onto another gravel path into woodland. At the next waymaked fork (post with No. 4 marked on it) go right, ignoring steps downwards after a few yards, and at the next post (No. 5), branch left around to a footbridge which you cross into a field.

Keep to the right edge of the field then loop left with the bottom boundary and, after a further 200 yards, do a little zigzag to continue the same course but on the other side of the boundary. At the end of the field turn 90 degrees right upwards between sparse trees and fence. When you reach the top of the incline you can see Oldbury Quarry to your left (not a pretty sight!). Try to forget it is there – over to your right are some good views to compensate. When you reach a stile do not cross it but stay left on the path you are following which broadens and takes you down to a gate by Quarry Farm where you exit onto a lane.

Turn right here then very shortly left at a junction along Steppy Lane which you stay on for about a mile, maybe slightly more. Almost immediately you get a view of the Coventry Canal across the fields on your right snaking its way through the valley and round Atherstone. An avenue of limes and beech trees presents a green haven until the quarry imposes itself on the landscape again. You pass the main entrance, where clearly the quarry company are at pains to make the appearance as unobtrusive as possible with restoration and planting schemes, and continue on past a few unusual looking properties ignoring all waymarks, including the one opposite Oldbury Farm. During the week you might get menaced by a few quarry vehicles along this lane but at weekends I would imagine it is fairly quiet. You go past Delamere Farm then look for a pool at lower level on your left. Shortly after this, but on the right, cross a waymarked stile into a field following the right boundary. ❶

Before the end of the field cross a stile and footbridge on the right and walk along the other side of the boundary towards what is left of a demolished cottage. Little more than a pile of bricks in fact. From there bear half right to the next waymark which you can see about 120 yards ahead. Cross a stile here and follow the direction half right towards a fir wood which you soon enter and follow a waymark left along the edge of the trees. A line of waymark posts through a new plantation leads you out onto a road where you turn left.

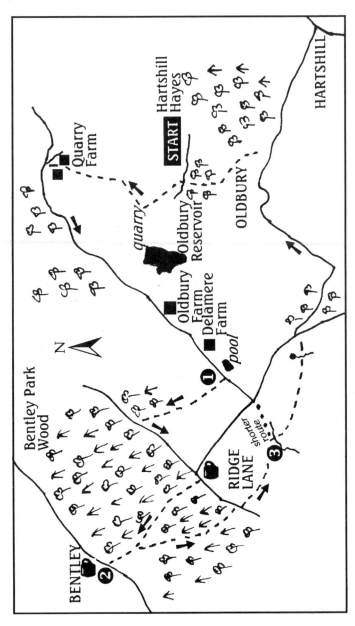

# Hartshill and Bentley

The road brings you into the village of Ridge Lane after about a third of a mile, passing the radio transmitter station you have been able to see for some time. If you are in dire need of refreshment at this point the White Hart might be a welcome sight, or you could even visit the Church End Brewery which brews its own ale, located in the main street between Nos 106 and 108 (open Fri, Sat, Sun only). Otherwise continue past the junction for about 30 yards before branching right at a waymark on a path into Bentley Park Wood. Keep on the main path through this pleasant mixed woodland for some two-thirds of a mile until reaching a waymark on your left. You don't need to do anything other than make a note of it at this stage as you will need to retrace your steps back to this point in due course. So, keep going until you exit the wood to find the Horse and Jockey directly opposite. ❷

When you can get a grip on yourself, leave the pub and retrace your steps to the waymark I referred to in the foregoing paragraph. Now follow the direction across an open field towards another part of the wood. Go with the waymark into the wood and keep ahead after a few yards at crosstracks then keep going along what can be a muddy path in parts right to the end where you cross a stile onto a road. The same road you walked along earlier but a different part of it, of course.

Cross the road and turn right and after 30 yards go left into The Rookery along Centenary Way*. Where the tarmac ends you continue ahead along the right side of a field and at the end of it bear left at a waymark along the adjacent edge. At the end of this long field is a kissing gate and a footbridge to negotiate. Those on the short route will now bear left but main walkers cross another footbridge immediately on the right. ❸

You now follow the right boundary of a field and, upon arriving at a farm, cross a stile by a gate on your right then turn left alongside farm buildings. On the other side of these cross the farm driveway and a stile on the other side into a field along the left edge. Immediately after passing a pool on your left look for a stile and footbridge on the right and, having crossed them, walk diagonally over a field to a waymark by a gate on the opposite side someway to the left of a group of houses. Exit onto a road turning left but after a few yards veer right along a lane signed Oldbury and Hartshill Hayes Country Park.

Keep going on the lane now for a little over a mile to arrive back at the Hartshill Hayes car park. Oh no, more road walking I can hear you say! However, this is a pretty little lane for the most part and takes you through some woodland and across a ridge with some decent views across towards Nuneaton, then twists and winds through the attractive settlement of Oldbury with its Victorian atmosphere before depositing you back at the starting point.

## Shorter Walk

Follow the main route from The Horse and Jockey, point (2) which involves crossing the road into the wood opposite to arrive at the waymark post referred to on your right after about a quarter of a mile. Continue the route now to point (3) where you turn left in front of a second footbridge. After walking along a field edge you go through gates on each side of a sewage works bounded by palisade fencing (it's not too bad – honest!) then down the right side of a field to exit onto a road via a gate.

Go straight across down Purley Chase Lane and after about 250 yards turn off left over a waymarked stile into a field. This is point (1) on the long route and you follow the directions from there back to the Horse and Jockey.

# 3

# Shustoke and Furnace End

## Fact*file*

**Maps:** Explorer 232; Landranger 139
**Distances:** Main walk 6.25 miles; shorter walks 3.75 or 3.25 miles.
**Main Start:** From the car park at Shustoke Reservoir, which is easy to find. The village itself is situated on the B4114, 2.5 miles to the north-east of Coleshill. GR 225908.
**Short Start:** The Griffin public house which is also on the B4114 one mile east of Shustoke. GR 243908. Alternatively, The Bulls Head at Furnace End which is almost a mile further along the road. GR 248913.
**Terrain:** Fairly easy going with a walk round Shustoke Reservoir to start you off, followed by a ramble cross country to Hoar Hall then return via Furnace End over pleasant countryside with some good views.

## The Pubs:

A walk where over indulgence could be tempting if you are not driving or are happy to become the subject of attention from the local constabulary.

**The Bulls Head, Furnace End:** A comfortable and friendly sixteenth century freehouse with the standard olde-worlde trappings, i.e. beamed ceilings, large Inglenook fireplace, little nooks and crannies. There is basically one large bar with a veranda type extension at the rear. A good selection of ale is on offer including Tetleys, Banks's, Bass, Worthington, Ansells, Church End, Guinness, Carlsberg and Carling. Bar snacks and restaurant meals specialising in Indian food. Open Mon-Sat 12-3 and 6-11; Sunday open all day from 12-10.30. Tel: 01675 481602

**The Griffin, Church End:** This has to be one of my all time favourite pubs – a real pub with a great atmosphere and great real beer. It's all a matter of personal preference I know but I really appreciate these days pubs which have retained their essential character and not been 'transformed' into theme pubs or other such style to become customised to modern trends. The building is clearly a mixture of architectural styles with the attractive seventeenth century frontage contrasting somewhat uncomfortably with the more modern extensions. Nevertheless, the interior is totally unspoilt with low beamed ceilings, fireplace and stone floors. It serves a magnificent array of real ales including Moby Dick, Landlord, Theakstons Old Peculier, Bombadier, Black Sheep, Grozet, Lager Celtic Ale, Pedigree and many others plus a host of various lagers and ciders. If you fancy something different try one of the country wines.

Another novelty is a selection of cheeses which are mainly of local origin. Apart from this, food is not served on a Sunday although it is on other days. There is a beer garden outside. Open Mon-Sat 12-2.30 and 7-11; Sun 12-2.30, 7-10.30. Tel: 01675 481205
There is also a third opportunity at the **Plough Inn** in Shustoke itself before finally arriving back at the car park.

The first part of the route is really easy and simply a walk around the west and east sides of the reservoir, which provides water supply for Coventry. As an information board will tell you, a scheme of tree planting and land management is being implemented to restore the land from two centuries of industrialisation and re-create the historic character of the area which inspired William Shakespeare.

You go clockwise around the Reservoir on the embankment path for a distance of a little over a mile to reach the eastern end where you go through a gate and turn immediately left down some steps and over a footbridge (signed Upper Reservoir). Negotiate the steps up the other side and proceed forward for a short distance before turning right to go clockwise round the Upper Reservoir, parallel with the railway line hidden in the trees to your left. Unfortunately you cannot get so close to the Upper Reservoir as you can the main reservoir. At the end turn right at a junction, away from the railway line, on a path which takes you to the left of a cottage along to another junction and waymark. Turn left here onto a broader track which is part of the Centenary Way*.

You go immediately right at a fork following waymarks on fence posts for Centenary Way and Heart of England Way*. You shortly come to a stile with another choice of routes and here take the left option, after which you soon cross another stile and walk out along the edge of a field. About 150 yards along divert left over a stile and under the rail track. You emerge to follow the line of a stream alongside a length of railing on your left around the edge of a field – do not be tempted to turn right on a path alongside the rail line. **❶**

Cross a footbridge on your left where there is another choice of routes. You will be relieved to learn that you are not required to take the option directly ahead through the middle of a large pool! Instead turn right to follow a course to the right of the pool, over a stile in a crossing boundary then another after a further 50 yards where the waymark sends you half left away from the stream across the centre of a field towards the next stile on the opposite side. You should be heading towards some houses and, once over this stile, continue forward along the bottom edge of a field and cross another stile about 80 yards ahead onto a path between the houses, which shortly brings you out onto the B4098.

Turn left here – best advice is to cross the road onto the footpath – but it is not long before you bear right along Pound Lane. Ignore a turning left but, shortly after that point where you reach the top of a rise by Fields Farm, go over a waymarked stile on the left and walk along the right boundary of a field. Cross another stile at the end with yet another choice. Proceed forward for about 15 yards before turning right over another stile which takes you into a field at the rear of the farm buildings. Please do not turn into the farmyard itself. Walk along the lower edge of the field with some nice views to the right towards the church spire of Over Whitacre. You reach and cross another stile before continuing the line but on the other side of the field boundary and exiting via a stile onto a narrow lane and turning right.

You quickly arrive at a junction with the B4116 and turn left, then immediately right, then immediately left at a fork along a concreted driveway. Please take care crossing the main road as you are right on a blind bend. You are now back on Centenary Way heading towards Hoar Hall. As you approach the property ignore a waymark on your left and stay on the driveway as it curves right. Just before a cattle grid in front of the farmyard turn 90 degrees left along a concreted roadway which swings right through a gate next to a slurry pit (well, they have to go somewhere!) down into a yard where you veer left through a swing gate then follow the concrete driveway between the buildings keeping right at a fork and passing to the left of the house. Regrettably there are no waymarks to guide you through here but hopefully you will not have too much trouble following my directions. ❷

Ignore a stile off to your left as the track swings round to the right through a swing gate from where you can appreciate the handsome classical lines of the Georgian building. At the end of the track you arrive at two gates with a stile between them; cross this into a field (beware, the ground around here can get

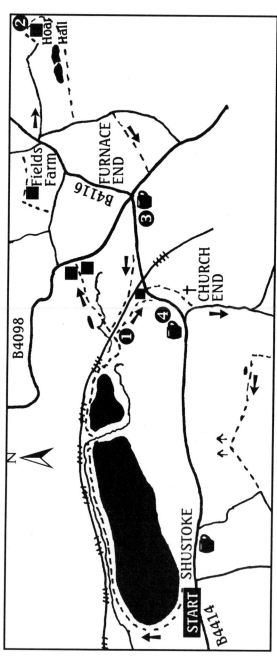

very muddy!) keeping to the right boundary then go over another stile into the next field to stay on the same line. There are some attractive pools on the right here which you may have spotted a little earlier when walking along the parallel path at higher level. At the end of this field is a further stile which you cross to continue on a driveway until exiting via a gate onto a lane where you turn left.

Stay on the lane for about 200 yards then look for a stile to cross on your right into a field to resume on the Centenary Way. Follow the left boundary and cross a stile into the adjoining field keeping the same line before crossing a further stile at the end onto the B4114 and turning right. A short distance will bring you to a crossroads in Furnace End where you bear left and the Bulls Head is just a few yards on the left. If you elect to patronise this hostelry do bear in mind that The Griffin is not very far away and a visit there is a real must. ❸

Go past the Bulls Head, or turn left on leaving, cross the road onto footpath and, after about 250 yards, go right at a Centenary Way waymark then keep to the left edge of a field around the rear of some workshops etc. At the end you arrive at point (1) again and turn left to go under the rail line for a second time. Cross a stile and bear left along the bottom edge of a field with a church in view off to the half right. The way loops right and exits onto the B4114 again where you turn left. You pass the entrance to a petroleum depot then turn off right through a kissing gate towards the church. In reality, as you might be aware, by sending you this way I have merely cut out a section of main road, which I always try to do even if it means walking a longer way round, as in this case. It is also easier to link up all three different variations of the walk.

Proceed up field to go through another kissing gate onto a driveway alongside the churchyard. You can visit the church of St. Cuthberts (see notes under Shustoke below) but it is, regrettably, kept locked. A notice in the porch tells you where the keys can be obtained. At the end of the driveway turn right to meet the main road again and you will come across The Griffin directly opposite. Cross the road carefully here as you are on a blind bend. ❹

If you are anything like me you will really have to tear yourself away from here and retreat back down the lane opposite but continue past the driveway to the church and past Church Farm and a gorgeous Old Rectory with one of the old style telephone boxes at the front. Ignore a turning left but take the next right. As this lane swings left after about 250 yards go right over a waymarked stile onto the Heart of England Way. Keep to the edge of a field and go through a gate into the next. At the end is another stile to cross with a choice of routes. Take the left option along a field edge and at the end cross a footbridge and stile to stay on line in the next field, with a pool now on your right.

At the end of this next field we depart from the H of E Way by going ahead over a stile along the right edge of the adjacent field. Cross two further stiles before walking along the edge of a wood. At the end of the wood divert right through an opening then bear immediately left along a grassy track then effectively continue ahead in the same field you were previously in. At the end go through a gap (there is evidence of the remains of a stile which has long since fallen into disuse) and continue ahead on a roughly surfaced driveway. You shortly cross a stile onto a residential lane and bear right. Turn left at a junction and left again on meeting the B4114 to regain the car park. As I said in the factfile, if you need a further injection of fluid the Plough is on your left before you get to the car park.

# Warwickshire Walks to Wet Your Whistle

*SHUSTOKE – the name of Dugdale is inextricably linked with the village and Sir William Dugdale of Blyth Hall owns much of the surrounding land and property. It remains very much a rural area although is well used to the influx of tourists, sailors and anglers visiting the reservoir. As indicated earlier you can visit the church of St Cuthbert which houses the tomb of a former Sir William Dugdale (b 1605), author of 'The Antiquities of Warwickshire' but you have to obtain a key. Until the mid seventeenth century the church was located within the village, as you would expect it to be, but the Plague decimated the population and the survivors moved away to form the basis of the present settlement. The Village Pound next to The Plough has recently been restored to its former glory.*

## Shorter Walks

### 1. From The Griffin, 3.75 miles.

Pick up the long route from point (4) and follow it to the end, i.e. the Shustoke Reservoir car park. Now start out on the long route down to point (1) but here turn right to follow the field edge adjacent to the rail line (do not go through the tunnel under the railway line). The way loops right to bring you out on the B4114 where you turn left past a petroleum depot then turn off right through a kissing gate towards the church. Now pick up the long route again from the paragraph before point (4) back to the start.

### 2. From the Bulls Head, 3.25 miles.

From point (3) pick up the long route which in fact returns to point (1) on its figure-of-eight shaped course and pick up the long route from there. You effectively turn right here (as opposed to left under the rail line) and walk along the adjacent field edge by a metal rail and now follow the long route back to the Bulls Head.

# 4

# Lapworth and Baddesley Clinton

---

## Fact*file*

**Maps:** Explorer 220 and 221; Landranger 139

**Distances:** Main walk 7.5 miles or 10.5 miles; shorter walk 4.5 miles

**Main Start:** Car park adjacent to Stratford-upon-Avon Canal in Broom Hall Lane, Lapworth, a turn off the B4439 running through the village just to the west of the point where it crosses the canal. Lapworth itself is located some six miles south-east of Solihull and eight miles north-west of Warwick. GR186710

**Short Start:** As above, the car park in Broom Hall Lane.

**Terrain:** A tremendously varied walk along a stretch of The Grand Union Canal, across pleasant agricultural land, through woods and, if you do the longest version, there are two superb National Trust Properties to visit. However, please see note below.

### The Pubs:

Again, this is one of those walks which incorporate several excellent hostelries and, if you had the time and inclination to sample them all, the resultant personality change might be noticed. (*There is a train service to Lapworth!*)

**The Boot Inn, Lapworth:** A rather 'up market' establishment which has been superbly refurbished to provide a real touch of class. Not a theme pub as such – better than that – with a re-created olde worlde atmosphere and a mouth-watering food menu. Perfectly OK for walkers (well, it would have to be with a name like The Boot) but you may feel a little out of place at times if you wade in with the full regalia and very muddy footwear – unless you can sit outside in the pleasant beer garden. There is a good selection of ales including Boddingtons, Old Speckled Hen, Wadsworths 6X, Heineken, Stella Artois, Guinness and Strongbow. Open Mon-Fri 11-3 and 5.30-11, Sat/Sun 11-11. Tel 01564 782464.

**The Tom O the Wood, Turner's Green:** More modern on the inside than it looks from without but, nevertheless, a most suitable watering hole with a beer garden and excellent bar menu. It consists basically of one large 'wrap around' bar and restaurant area with a conservatory extension. Good selection of ales including Old Toms, Tetley, HSB, Wadsworths XXL, Old Speckled Hen, Heineken, Stella Artois, Guinness and Scrumpy Jack. Open all day every day. Tel 01564 782252.

**The Case is Altered, Five Ways (Haseley):** Full of olde-worlde character this free house has a unique, even eccentric, ambience and is a must if you want to experience something a little out of the ordinary. There is a bar and a lounge, the former having a stone floor and an open fireplace, with a little beer garden in between. Serving Hook Norton and Brains Dark Mild plus guest beers, Guinness and Lager. Open Mon-Fri 12-2.30 and 6-11, Sat 11.30-2.30 and 6-11, Sun 12-2 and 7-10.30. No meals served. Tel: 01926 484206

**The Navigation, Lapworth:** As the name implies this is a canal side pub (M&B) and offers Ginger Tom, Brew XI, Bass, Worthington, Woodpecker, Strongbow and Carling. Good for walkers, having a stone floored bar. Restaurant and pleasant beer garden alongside canal. Open Mon-Fri 11-2.30 and 5.30-11, Sat/Sun all day. Tel: 01564 783337

**The Punch Bowl, Lapworth:** A more modern type of pub than the others although built in an old style and somewhat more family orientated. Nevertheless, it has a pleasant interior and may be a welcome watering hole on a warm day. It is a Banks's pub and you can take you pick from Pedigree, Guinness, Stella Artois plus usually a guest beer. Food available. Beer Garden. Open Mon-Sat 11.30-11 and Sun 12-10.30. Tel: 01564 784564

**Please note**

I would suggest you give consideration to the timing of this walk. Bearing in mind the distances and amount of interest involved it is highly unlikely that you will have sufficient time to complete the longest version and take in both National Trust properties (*see opening times in text*). If you want to do everything full justice, including the great pubs *en route*, it would be much more practical to make two separate visits.

A t the rear of the car park is a pretty canal basin with locks and some unusual canalside cottages. You are in fact at Kingswood Junction where the Stratford-upon-Avon* and the Grand Union* Canals meet, although they go off again in their separate directions.

Turn right and cross over a small bridge and follow the path signed Grand Union Canal to cross another little bridge by a barrel roof cottage. These unusual buildings are a feature of the southern part of the waterway – it has been suggested that the cottages were built this way for cheapness and that the men who constructed the canal tunnels could easily put up a cottage in this form. You keep following the sign to the Grand Union and walk along an arm of water linking the two canals, which is lined with moored houseboats, to shortly reach the junction with the Grand Union. Here turn right onto the towpath and follow it under bridge No. 64 then down to the next bridge at Turner's Green. It is a pity that the tranquillity of this section of the canal is blighted by the constant noise of traffic on the M40 which runs nearby but we will soon leave that behind. Indeed, if you need compensation you are already at the first *en route* pub. You can see a former warehouse on the opposite side where goods were loaded and unloaded for the mill behind. The mill is now the Tom O the Wood pub and I don't think you will need detailed directions to find it but please note that it does not open until noon.

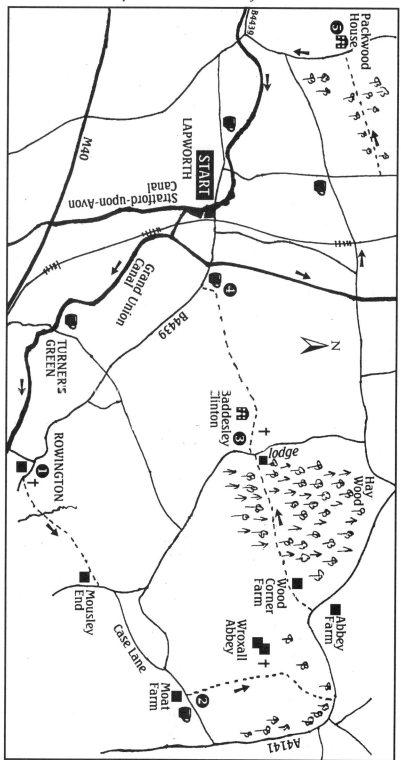

If you do make the stop, as you have barely started the walk I trust you will not encounter any problems departing. Return to the towpath until you reach the next bridge No.62 – go under it then turn sharp right up an embankment, cross a stile and turn right over the bridge. You are now on a short section of lane which takes you alongside the walled boundary to Culvers Hill before coming out at a junction in the village of Rowington. **1**

*Tom O The Wood*

*ROWINGTON has its foundations in Saxon times when it was a fragmented woodland village in what was then part of the Forest of Arden. It has a number of interesting buildings, not the least of which is the Elizabethan Shakespeare Hall – yet another local building with connections to the Bard's family. We are not quite sure which part though! Much of its past prosperity was owed to the nearby stone quarry, now disused, material from which was used in the building of not only the parish church but St. Philip's Cathedral in Birmingham and Baddesley Clinton Hall. Unlike some other villages in the county, Rowington has resisted temptations to become another commuter village and remains a tucked away outpost of rural life with many of the farms remaining in families having long associations with it. Long may it be so.*

Cross the road and turn right as if to go downhill but immediately enter the churchyard via a flight of steps and turn right onto a path which runs above the road. Unfortunately, the church was locked at the time of my visit, as are so many now in order to protect their contents from plunder. A sad manifestation of modern society. At the rear boundary cross a stile then the bottom section of a field diagonally to the left corner (or is it right – another one of those conundrums!) where you walk through into the adjacent field and along the short bottom boundary before crossing a stile into the next field. Cross this open field directly on the same line to cross another stile (when you get there you will find that it is in fact a footbridge) which you can see on the far side.

Once across you are faced with another open field and you need to turn half left across it to a marker post under a bushy tree you can see at the end of the top boundary coming in from the right. At the time of research this field was cropped but the farmer had marked the way across, for which I was grateful

18

and hopefully this will be the case should you be doing this walk in the growing season. At the marker post curve round to the right to follow the field edge with a mixed tree boundary on your right on a gentle upward climb which brings you to another stile. Cross this into the next field and at the end go over a further stile by gates onto a lane.

On your right here is the most attractive farmhouse called Mousley End which appears to date from Elizabethan times. However, we need to go left and then shortly fork right along Case Lane. Ignore a stile on the left and another on the right shortly afterwards and keep going past a left turn. You ignore a further waymark left on reaching a residential area but, after passing Moat Farm on your right, you will need to take the next path on your left waymarked Wroxall Abbey. Before doing so you might wish to visit the second pub a short distance further along the lane with the intriguing name of The Case Is Altered. I asked the barman if he knew the origin of the name but he said 'no', probably because he was fed up with every other customer asking the same question!

**❷**

Do not slip into a state of total inertia as there is still some way to go. On leaving, backtrack the short distance to the path signed Wroxall Abbey and cross a small field and the stile on the opposite side and continue ahead adjacent to a strip of trees. At the end cross a stile and walk alongside a brick wall and on to the driveway to the Abbey, which you cannot fail to have noticed over to your left. This splendid building, now a private school, is English Heritage Grade II classified and was once owned by Sir Christopher Wren. There is an historic fourteenth century priory church attached. Where the driveway curves left you should stay ahead to go through a gate into a field where there is a fascinating section of brick wall which includes the original carriage entrance at the end of an avenue of oak trees, which I believe originate from the late seventeenth century. Keep ahead in the field parallel to the avenue of oaks and to the left of a pond through attractive parkland. You reach a waymark in a crossing boundary and turn right onto a gravel track heading towards a wood. At the end go through a gate then over a stile by another gate to exit onto the A4141 and turn left.

Unfortunately, you have to walk along the main road for about half a mile but there is a footpath on the other side. As you get near to Abbey Farm, which you have been able to see for some time, cross the road again and turn off left along a waymarked driveway ending at Wood Corner Farm.

Go through the entrance gate then bear immediately left in front of the rather gorgeous black and white timbered property before swinging right through another gate at the rear of some farm buildings to yet another which leads you into a field. Turn half right cutting off the corner of the field to go through a waymarked gate located in a kink in the boundary to Hay Wood.

Once through you immediately keep left at a fork onto a narrow path in mixed woodland (Forestry Commission). Please be warned – parts of the path get very muddy in or after wet weather! The presence of marsh grass is a telling sign. Go straight ahead on reaching a broad crossing track, after which conifers become more predominant and eventually exit the wood via a gate by the Old Keeper's Lodge onto a gravel driveway. The driveway soon exits onto a lane where you turn left then immediately right on another driveway signed Baddesley Clinton. On arrival at a gate go through and, if you wish to visit St. Michael's Church you can do so at this point, otherwise or afterwards go through another gate to continue on the gravel path, which takes you up to the manor house of Baddesley Clinton itself (National Trust). ❸

*If you do visit the church you will find that it is a place of considerable beauty which has its roots in the thirteenth century. It fell into disrepair in the nineteenth century but was restored in 1872 and again in the 1960s at the cost of Thomas Ferrers, Lord of the Manor of Baddesley Clinton. There are a number of interesting features including a Sarah Green Chamber Organ, an oak rood screen, some superb stained glass and various tombs, mainly of the Ferrers family. There is a leaflet available providing further detail.*

*The Manor House, which is described as 'romantic and atmospheric', dates from 1438 and is little changed from the mid seventeenth century. The Elizabethan interior boasts a number of interesting features including a series of armorial windows depicting marriage alliances through the centuries, fine heraldic chimney pieces, a private chapel and three priest-holes, thus becoming a refuge for persecuted Catholics. It was owned by the Ferrers family for 500 years; they were of Norman and Royal descent and fervent Royalists during the Civil War. It passed into the care of The National Trust in 1980. The grounds, which are part of the ancient Forest of Arden, are delightful and offer lake and nature walks. Licensed restaurant. Open (2003) 5 March – 2 Nov daily except Mons & Tues (open BH Mons), 1.30-5.30. The grounds only are open 5 March – 14 Dec on the same days of the week from 12 noon to 5.30 or 4.30 Nov/Dec. Admission £6.00; family £15. Grounds and restaurant only £3.00. You can buy a combined ticket for Baddesley Clinton and Packwood House at a discount to the individual prices. Tel: 01564 783294*

When you have completed your visit, or even if choosing not to do so, you need to effectively execute a right turn at the end of the gravel path referred to above, past the entrance to the car park onto the main access drive for vehicles. After a short distance look for a stile on your left taking you into a field along the right side of the house and follow a course through it parallel to the wicket fence to the grounds on your left. You gradually close with the fence and, at the end of the field, cross another stile by a National Trust sign. If you were not already aware of it you are now walking a section of The Heart of England Way*. There is a little brook to negotiate after the stile and you now continue ahead along the left boundary of the ensuing field, cross another stile at the end of it and, in the next field, veer slightly away from the left boundary towards the left of a brick and tile building you can see a little to the right.

When you get there cross a waymarked stile and bear right through a stable yard and out over another stile onto a gravel drive which shortly exits onto the B4439. Turn right to find The Navigation. ❹

You will not, I trust, have imbibed here as well as the three previous pubs otherwise I think you will definitely not be in the mood to complete the optional extension to the long walk – a further three miles or so. If you wish to finish now, and perhaps save the rest for another day, turn right on leaving the pub then cross the bridge and the road to go left down steps onto the towpath of the Grand Union Canal. Turn right, away from the bridge, and on reaching the 'arm' section traversed on the outward route, cross the bridge and turn right onto it before reversing your steps back to the car park.

If you have the time and inclination to go the full distance turn left on reaching the towpath to go under the bridge and walk along a long, straight section of canal for about three-quarters of a mile and, at the next bridge

# Lapworth and Baddesley Clinton

(No.66) leave the towpath by going up the embankment and turning left on meeting a lane. This takes you through a residential area and you pass Station Lane, after which the footpath ends so a little care is required from here. You cross a railway bridge and in another quarter of a mile reach a crossroads where you turn right down Chessetts Wood Road. However, I am sure that you will not have failed to notice yet another pub opposite, called The Punch Bowl. If you are dying of thirst or haven't yielded to previous temptation, give it a try.

Chessetts Wood Road is a very smart residential area and, after ignoring all waymarked paths on your right, take the one on your left over a stile, just past the entrance to Uplands Farm. You are greeted by another National Trust sign and walk along an avenue of mixed trees, mainly oak and lime in changing profusion. You cross a stile into a small wood followed by another one upon exiting, where there is a choice of routes.

We continue along the avenue to arrive directly opposite Packwood House and you go through a gate and down some steps onto a lane running in front of the property. **5**

*Packwood House is a unique twentieth century re-creation of domestic Tudor architecture although it incorporates the original sixteenth century timber framed farmhouse (the timbers have now been rendered over). It was owned by the Fetherstone family who where a little duplicitous in their allegiances during and just after the Civil War. The Parliamentarian General Henry Ireton slept there before the battle of Edge Hill (see walk No. 22 in Walks through History in the Heart of England) and it is said that Charles II was given food and drink here after his defeat at Worcester in 1651. The interior, created by Graham Baron Ash between the two world wars contains many fine examples of sixteenth century furniture and artefacts some of which were purchased from Baddesley Clinton when the fortunes of the Ferrers family were at a low ebb. The gardens have a famous collection of yew trees laid out in the seventeenth century to represent 'The Sermon on the Mount'. Open (2003) 5 Mar-2 Nov daily except Mons & Tues (open BH Mons) 12–4.30. Garden open on the same days, 11.00-5.30 or 4.30 in Mar, April & Oct. Admission £5.40, family £13.50. Garden only £2.70. <u>You can buy a combined ticket for Packwood House and Baddesley Clinton at a discount to the individual prices.</u> Tel: 01564 783294*

Turn left on the lane, or right after visiting the House, and stay on this for about two-thirds of a mile. Keep right at the first junction but, on reaching the second, go left to meet the B4439. Immediately cross the road and bridge, turning right onto the canal towpath then right again under the bridge. You come to a lock which is No 6 in a long flight of 19 taking you back to Kingswood Junction. At lock No 7 you have to cross a bridge to continue on the towpath on the other side of the canal and you cross back again at No. 14. I stopped a while here to watch a narrowboat working its way through this tortuous flight of locks and thought that this type of activity could only be suitable for relaxed personalities with a lot of patience for it must take hours to get through the whole system. I suppose boaters accept it as part of the enjoyment but I think I would get increasingly impatient with each lock. If you go through the gateway on your right here you can gain access through the car park to the Boot Inn, an exceptionally good establishment if you fancy yet another drink. Surely not though, unless you are actually just doing the short walk or are a total inebriate.

Continue on the towpath through another lock system between bridges 34 and 35 and on back to the car park.

## Shorter Walk

*The shorter walk takes in the National Trust property of Packwood House, details of which are provided in the text.*

From the car park follow the long route to the junction with the Grand Union Canal. Turn left here on the towpath for a short wander up to the first road bridge, where you can leave the canal to visit the Navigation Pub if you wish, point (4) – see Factfile for details.

If not stopping just continue along the towpath or, if you are stopping, return to it afterwards and pick up the long walk from the paragraph after point (4) and follow it all the way back to the car park.

*Packwood House*

# 5

# Thurlaston and Frankton

## Fact*file*

**Maps:** Explorer 222; Landranger 140 & 151
**Distances:** Main Walk 6.25 miles; shorter walk 3.25 miles
**Main Start:** The village of Thurlaston which is easily reached just to the south of the junction of the M45 and A45, about four miles south-west of Rugby centre and close by Draycote Water. There is parking space in the main street by the telephone box. GR 467709
**Short Start:** The Friendly Inn at Frankton which is a little further to the west and accessed via the B4453 running off the A45. GR 426704
**Terrain:** A pleasant ramble over undulating countryside with some good views across Draycote Water and elsewhere. No climbs of any significance.
NB The walk does not take in any of the path around the Water itself but you can get down to the shore from Thurlaston if you want to get a closer look – see note at end of walk.

## The Pub:

**The Friendly Inn, Frankton:** An attractive hostelry which certainly has a name to live up to – and it does! There is a bar and lounge serving Green King, Abbot Ale, IPA, Tiger, Ruddles, XS Smooth, Carlsberg, Stella Artois, Guinness, Woodpecker and Strongbow ciders. Bar snacks available and a restaurant serving meals but no food on Mondays or Sunday evenings. Outside seating. Open 12-3 and 6-11. Tel: 01926 632430

Start the walk by continuing down the main street which is a No Though Road, past Church Lane and the delightfully named Pudding Bag Lane. Shortly after the latter go through a kissing gate on your right which is situated just behind a tree planted to celebrate the Royal Wedding in 1981. A lot of water has gone under the bridge since then, hasn't it? You should now be on a path between hedgerows and private gardens. Cross a stile to proceed on a grassy path to the left of a fence then a private pool where there is a rather intimidating sign 'Beware of the crocodile, trespassers will be eaten!' If you survive, continue on the same line to the left of a fence into a paddock from where you exit via a stile onto a lane and turn left. You pass a farm on your right opposite which you catch a glimpse of Draycote Water before coming to a golf course on your right.

*The reservoir was completed in 1970 and at full capacity covers more than 600 acres, holds 5,000 million gallons of water and is 65ft deep at its deepest point. Unlike many reservoirs, Draycote has not been created by damming a river but instead is a storage reservoir which is filled by pumping water from the*

# Warwickshire Walks to Wet Your Whistle

*River Leam during the winter months – helping to reduce the risk of floods. During summer it is pumped to Rugby and also released back into the Leam, which is used as an aqueduct, to carry the water to Leamington. The reservoir supports a wide variety of waterfowl and one of the county's Country Parks is located on the southern edge, accessed from the A426.*

When you pass the entrance to Grange Farm go forward through a waymarked gate onto a broad vehicle track going across the golf course, so beware of flying balls! Where the track veers left to a field barn, go straight

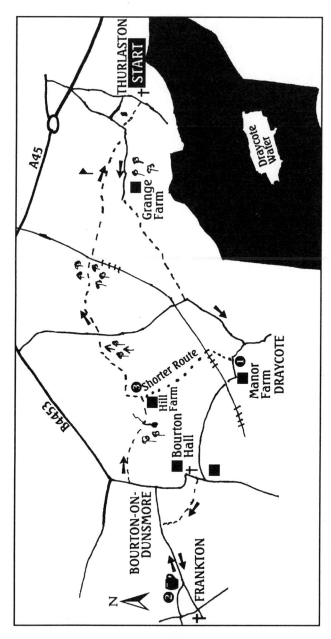

ahead on a grassy track through a gate into a field where you keep to the right edge to negotiate another gate at the end before exiting onto a path between hedgerows. The path ends at an open field where you walk along the left side on a defined path but, where the hedgeline kinks left, continue the line forward across the centre of the field to exit via a gate onto a lane where you turn left.

A walk of about half a mile will bring you into the village of Draycote. You pass a couple of attractive farmhouses after which the lane loops left and is joined by a pretty brook. On reaching a junction turn right and, after maybe 100 yards or so, you will reach a stile on your right which is where those on the shorter walk join the route. **❶**

Stay on the lane past Manor Farm and onwards for another third of a mile to arrive at St. Peters church at Bourton-on-Dunsmore, which was unfortunately locked at the time of my visit. As you walk along, the elevations of Bourton Hall impose themselves on your right and just as you get to the church at the top of the hill take a breather on the bench conveniently placed to provide a splendid view across Draycote Water towards the Cotswolds in the distance. The hall was built in the late eighteenth century and ceased to be a private home in 1947 and, after a period when it was used as a school, it was purchased by Ingersoll Engineers for conversion to a workplace. The word Bourton, incidentally, is derived from the Anglo-Saxon 'Bor' a hill and 'Dun' a town. I imagine, therefore, that this was once a larger settlement relatively speaking than it is today.

You can walk through the church precincts to exit via a gate on the far side. You now have a choice; turn right along the lane and through the pretty village of Bourton-on-Dunsmore or track across fields to 'cut off the corner'. If opting for the latter skip to the start of the next paragraph. If taking the village route you will soon pass the entrance to Bourton Hall (now converted to office use) and follow the lane as it winds its way between a number of interesting

*Bourton Church*

properties to reach a left turn to Frankton. Follow this now into the village and The Friendly Inn after a further half-mile. **2**

Those opting for the field route should cross the road directly on emerging from the church precincts to go down a waymarked path between houses and emerge into a field. Your direction is slightly right across the field to a gap you can see on the far boundary, although you may wish to consider walking around the edge to the same point. Go through and proceed straight across the next field to a waymark post you can see on the opposite side. This takes you onto a grassy path at the end of which you bear right at a crossing track and along a short section of field to exit onto a lane and turn left. Follow the lane now for about a third of a mile into Frankton where you will have no trouble in finding the Friendly Inn. **2**

*The Friendly Inn*

Don't get too friendly otherwise continuation of the walk might prove a less than attractive proposition. When you leave you may wish to look around the village and possibly visit the church which is reached by continuing down the lane just beyond the main part of the village. There is information inside about its history and that of prominent local families for those interested. Otherwise or afterwards, retrace your steps past the point of earlier access onto the incoming lane and, ignoring all waymarks on the right, turn left when you reach a junction. Continue past the first waymark on the right but, about 150 yards before you reach the next junction, go through an open gap on your right (opposite a sports pitch) into a field. Stay by the right edge and keep with it as it swings right through a gap. This is a very long field and, although the landscape is flat, it is not totally unattractive. At the end of the field loop left with the bottom boundary for just a few yards before turning right to cross a footbridge into the adjoining field. Now go straight ahead cutting off the bottom corner to meet and turn left along the side boundary heading towards a farm. When you get to the farm go straight ahead on a driveway between buildings to reach a waymarked gate on your left. There is a good long distance view of Draycote Water from this point. **3**

Go through the gate and along the left field boundary to a waymark in the corner where you bear right along the adjacent edge of the same field to join a surfaced track going away from the farm. It will not escape your notice that the same track cuts diagonally across the field to the same point but I am telling you the official route. It will also not escape your notice that there is another view of Draycote Water from here. The track brings you out at a lane which you cross directly following a waymark through a gate into a field then turn half left to walk across to a post which you can see underneath a tree on the left boundary. On reaching this point bear right along the said boundary down to the end.

Here cross a footbridge and go ahead across an open field towards a wood on the far side – you will shortly see a waymark post in front of the wood to guide you. Once in the wood you need to cross a couple of footbridges with care and emerge to climb some steps to a stile. Cross this and the line of the unused railway to find yourself back on the golf course! Take a little care over direction here. You need to walk ahead across part of the course circumventing a pool to join and continue along the right of a hedge. The way is quite well marked so you should not have any difficulty – if you do then I'm sure the golfers will put you right. Keep going as far as you can until the boundary kinks right, where you cross a double stile into an open field.

Now this is where I will sing the praises of Warwickshire County Council and their waymarking excellence. Throughout the County, with a few minor exceptions, the waymarking has been far above the standard of some other authorities and the point at hand is no exception. Once over the stiles continue straight ahead across the field for about 50 yards to reach an electricity pole with a waymark on it directing you 90 degrees right heading towards the left edge of some trees. In my experience this is just the sort of situation where the waymarks would just peter out leaving you wondering exactly which is the correct path, but not so here. As it is though you may be obliged to think about walking round the edge of the field if it is cropped and a path across is not marked out.

The course takes you towards a farm on your right which you actually passed on the other side on the outward route. Hopefully you will find a waymarked stile in the jutting in corner of a paddock, behind which are some corrugated metal farm buildings. Cross the stile and keep to the left side of the paddock and go over a stile at the far side adjacent to the farm buildings referred to. Cross a farm track through a gateway adjacent to barns and onto a grassy track and exit via a stile onto a lane after about 40 yards. Turn left on the lane and follow it back into Thurlaston.

To get down to the Water go down Church Lane and, where it swings left, go straight on through a waymarked gate and follow the concreted path to the bottom, where you go through a kissing gate and over a footbridge to reach the roadway which goes round the reservoir.

*Thurlaston – a little uncertainty seems to exist regarding the origin of the name! One source suggests it derives from the Viking Thorstein's Tun but another states that it was known as Torlawestone before assuming its present name. Can anyone say with authority which is correct? Whichever, the village is on a no through route and, therefore, has a quiet, peaceful ambience. It boasts a number of interesting buildings, not the least of which is St.Edmund's church. It is relatively modern, having been completed in 1848 and originally designed for use as the village school and has a most unusual tower (which was originally taller than it is now) which houses living accommodation, formerly for a schoolmaster at the school. The rope to the bell turret passes through one of the rooms – not so good on Sundays if you are non- churchgoer! The stained glass window is striking and was installed very recently in 1997. Have a walk around this delightful village.*

## Shorter Walk

Starting from the Friendly Inn at Frankton, point (2), follow the long route to point (3) and the gate on your left. Do not follow the long route by turning left through it but go right along to the rear of the farm buildings and out into a field. Walk alongside the timber fence as it kinks right to meet the right boundary of the field which you then follow downwards to a gate at the bottom. Go through the gate then forwards across the next field on the same line about 40 yards parallel from the right boundary to reach a stile in the bottom boundary. The field was planted at the time of my visit but the farmer had marked a path through. Why can't they all do that, it would make life a lot easier for walker and farmer alike?

Cross the stile and go under a bridge carrying a disused railway line (the former Rugby to Leamington line closed in 1958) before bearing right in a pasture field. Do not keep to the fence line along the base of the railway embankment but veer away from it to cross the field section diagonally to a point at the end of a line of trees on the left boundary. When you get there continue the same line across another field section to a stile in the boundary about 80 yards to the right of a pretty black and white cottage. Cross the stile and turn right on a lane. This is point (1) on the long walk and you now follow the text through and back to the Friendly Inn.

# 6

# Tanworth-in-Arden and Ullenhall

## Fact*file*

**Maps:** Explorer 220; Landranger 139
**Distances:** Main walk 8 miles; shorter walk 4.5 miles
**Main start:** Anywhere convenient in Tanworth-in-Arden. There are normally parking spaces available in the village centre, which is easily accessible from M42 J3 (then via A435) about four miles to the north-west or from the south via the A4189 from Redditch or Henley-in-Arden and through Ullenhall. GR 113705.
**Short start:** The Winged Spur at Ullenhall, which is located off the B4189 between Redditch and Henley-in-Arden. GR 122674
**Terrain:** Easy walking along well signed paths in gentle countryside. Some pleasant views and no climbs worth mentioning.

## The Pub:

**The Winged Spur** in Ullenhall is a classic traditional village pub which has been opened up into one large room – with cosy nooks and corners. The ceiling is supported by huge timbers and brick pillars which, together with three real fires, give the pub a comfortable ambience. There are various slogans posted on the walls and beams such as 'The only way to entertain some folks is to listen to them'. The pub has associations with the old Ullenhall family of Knight of nearby Barrells Hall (now a ruin) who chose the Spur, symbol of medieval Knighthood, as the family crest. A Real Ale pub serving Boddingtons, Caffreys, Flowers, IPA, Whitbread Mild, Stella Artois, Guinness, Heineken and Stowford Press Cider. At the time of my visit the guest ale was Weatheroak, brewed locally in Alvechurch. Bar snacks and meals. Outside seating. Opening times, Mon-Sat 12-11, Sun 12-10.30. Tel: 01564 792005

*TANWORTH-in-ARDEN. This picturesque village has pre-Norman roots and was located within the Forest of Arden, which covered most of central Warwickshire in Medieval times. The 'in Arden' bit was actually added in the nineteenth century for postal convenience. It has a classic village green which is only spoilt by parked cars (that's the price we pay for modern convenience) and an interesting church originating from the fourteenth century. It was substantially renovated by the Victorians and is little altered from that time. The stained glass is superb with each window commemorating a benefactor and there is also a huge wooden chest which pre-dates the church itself. The churchyard contains the grave of Nick Drake who died in 1974 and has a cult following for his eerie folk music. Today, Tanworth is very much a commuter village, like many others in the area, although it has managed to retain its old character by dint of effort by the Village Preservation Society.*

# Warwickshire Walks to Wet Your Whistle

Walk along the main street away from the church and, on rounding the bend, turn off left down Bates Lane and through a pleasant residential area. Stay on the lane as it swings left and descends but, just as it starts to rise again, cross a waymarked stile on your left into a field. Keep to the left edge following the course of a brook and when you reach some barns circumvent them to the right and go over a stile onto a lane. Cross the lane directly over another stile and walk along the right edge of a field towards Oakwood Farm ahead. When you get there you need to divert right over a stile next to the first barn to pass to the right of them all to cross another stile by a gate at the end. After literally only a few yards and before reaching the farmhouse turn right through a waymarked gate onto a broad track.

This track curves around the rear of the farmhouse where you arrive at a junction of paths and you now veer left across a stile just before a house and over another stile into an open field. (At the time of writing the house, originally derelict, had been renovated and the garden was being constructed so there may be some minor changes here). Bear half right in the field towards a line of (mainly) oak trees heading for the largest one down in a dip, underneath which is a stile to cross into the adjacent field. The right boundary of this field very shortly swings right to take you on a rising course to another stile under another oak tree. Once over this bear slightly left towards a line of trees on the far

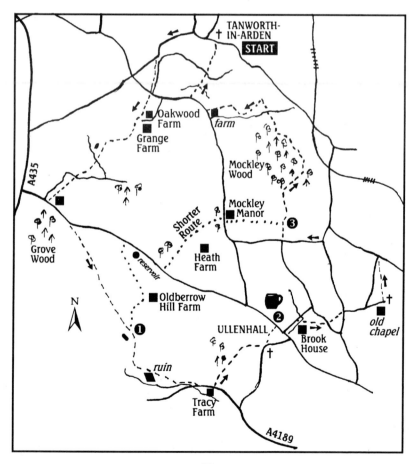

30

boundary of the next field, ignoring a stile on the right, then continue with the tree line downfield with an attractive fishing pool to your right, which can be better seen when the trees end.

When you reach the bottom, cross a stile and follow the waymark right down to a plank footbridge which looks as though it has passed its sell-by date. However, it appeared sound at the time of my visit although it might be easier to cross the brook itself! Once over cross another stile into the next field and continue in it with the boundary on your right for just a short distance to where it swings right. At this point continue the line forward across the open field, cross a stile in a crossing boundary and stay on line towards the bottom corner of the next field gradually closing with the tree line on your left. When you get there cross a fence stile and a plank footbridge (please take care as the timber can get slippery) to follow the waymark left across another footbridge (which can also get slippery) before turning right in the ensuing field. This is quite a large thistly field and you keep the tree lined brook on your right until exiting onto a lane via a stile about 100 yards in from the top right corner.

Don't take the inviting looking stile opposite but turn left along the lane in front of some cottages. You shortly join a wide grass verge and cross over the driveway to Grovewood House before crossing a footbridge on your right, just before the verge narrows to a point. You will find yourself in a field and should cross to the right boundary and follow it until approximately halfway down before crossing a stile on your right and continuing the line but now to the right of the boundary. Some nice views open up ahead and, on a clear day, you can see the Cotswolds in the distance. Go through a gap in a crossing boundary to continue the course in the next, large, field and at the end cross a stile into another large field. When you reach the end go through a waymarked gate and stay on line in another largish field. Partway along the short route comes in via a gate on the left. ❶

Keep going until passing through a gate by a sunken pool. At the end of the next field cross a stile then go through a waymarked gap at the end of the next, and into a field where you can see a walled ruin ahead. Pass to the left of the ruin and at the bottom of the field you are channelled onto a narrow path between small trees adjacent to a brook. You very shortly cross a footbridge, the area around which can get boggy, and proceed adjacent to the left boundary of the ensuing field which soon curves round the garden of a smart residence to a stile which you go over onto the driveway to the house. Cross that into the field opposite where you follow the same line but a short distance out from the left boundary. A stile at the end will bring you out onto the A4189 where you turn left. I would suggest that you cross the road onto the broad grass verge opposite. You quickly pass a golf club workshop and arrive at Tracy Farm next to it, at which point re-cross the road and go over the stile directly opposite into a small plantation.

Walk along the left edge of the plantation and at the end turn right through a gap to cross a double stile into a field which you traverse directly cutting off the bottom right corner heading for the right edge of a wood. You walk along the edge of the wood and go through a waymarked gate before turning left over a stile at the end of the wood then right to stay on the same line but now to the left of the boundary hedge. Cross a little plank footbridge and a stile into the next field where you stay on the line with the houses of Ullenhall now in view. After the boundary kinks right cross a stile and the following field diagonally to the bottom right corner where you can see another waymark on an oak tree. Cross a stile here then turn left, then immediately right, over another stile into Church Road.

Turn left and you shortly arrive at the church of St. Mary the Virgin, which has a gorgeous interior with a timber vaulted roof designed to resemble the hull of a boat. It is only about 125 years old and contains some fascinating memorials, including one to a member of the Throckmorton family of Coughton Court who was executed at Tyburn in the reign of Mary Queen of Scots. Directly opposite the church go through a kissing gate and cut straight across a field to join a paling fence and through another kissing gate taking you between houses out into the village of Ullenhall. It will not escape your notice that the Winged Spur is right opposite. **❷**

*The Winged Spur*

*ULLENHALL. Another picturesque village which has remained relatively unspoilt despite its proximity to Birmingham and major transport routes. Like its neighbour Tanworth, however, there is a feeling of unrest because of the process of 'edging out' of the locals by the affluent commuters. Nearby Barrells Hall was the home of Henrietta, Lady Luxborough, in the first part of the eighteenth century – she was the first wife of Robert Knight, Earl of Catherlow, and it was there that she gathered a literary circle which included the poets William Somerville and Jago of Beaudesert, amongst others. Ullenhall subsequently became the spiritual home of writers who, at that time, were struggling to come to terms with the scientific and engineering advances which were having such a profound effect on attitudes of the people. The Hall was seriously damaged by fire in 1933 and remains a ruin, although Lady Luxborough is said to haunt them. Perhaps the most interesting building is the Old Chapel and you will see that shortly.*

Having overcome any urge to linger for a serious length of time, turn left on leaving then keep left at a fork by War Memorial and at road junction bear left along a very pretty lane bordering a brook. You actually need to take the elevated path alongside a metal rail fence and Brook House and go through a wicket gate before turning right along the lower edge of a field at the rear of the house, joining the Arden Way*. Where the fence kinks right continue directly ahead slicing off the bottom corner of the field to exit via a gate onto a narrow lane. Cross this up some steps and through a kissing gate to walk across the next field roughly down the centre on a well walked line and exit via another kissing gate onto another lane.

Go ahead across the junction into Chapel Lane. To avoid any doubt the first building you pass on the right is called Kingthorpe Lodge. Keep right at a fork and where the tarmac ends continue ahead through a gate to arrive at the Old Chapel. This tiny, magical, thirteenth century building was originally the chancel of a larger church and is currently the subject of a restoration appeal. There is an information panel in the chapel so I will not go into great detail here, but do visit – it is an enchanting place. On leaving, retreat to the Old Chapel Cottage and directly opposite cross a stile into a field turning right along the top edge of it. However, you soon depart from that line to follow a line of oaks across the field to exit via a stile to arrive at a junction of roads. Turn left at the junction – do not go through the waymarked gate opposite- down a single track lane.

Continue on the lane and bear left at a junction then right after about 40 yards along a lane signed Ullenhall with the delightful name of Gentleman's Lane. This takes you through a very 'up market' area and, on reaching a left turn to Ullenhall, cross a stile opposite which is hidden in a hedgerow. Now head directly across a field and go over a stile by a gate on the opposite boundary. There is a choice of routes here and which way you go will depend upon whether you are taking the short or the long walk. Those on the short route will go ahead along the left boundary and the leg stretchers will veer a little right along the right boundary. ❸

At the end of the field cross a stile onto a broad track between high fences and on over another stile, after which the path narrows to take you through a

*Old Chapel in Ullenhall*

section of Mockley Wood. A word of warning here – sections of this path can get overgrown and muddy so I hope you are suitably attired! The path goes around to the left and winds along the bottom edge of the wood with the railway line now for company over to your right. Eventually the path comes to a halt and you are obliged to go through a waymarked gate into a field.

You circumvent a pool then continue parallel to the right boundary of the field and at the end cross a stile and footbridge to stay ahead on a broad rising track. Almost at the top of the rise you reach a junction of paths with a waymarked gate and another to the left of it. Go through the first gate then turn sharp left through the other to walk along the right edge of the adjoining field. At the end go through gates and continue ahead on a track to the right of a post and wire fence. The track ends at a field corner, or more accurately swings right then left through a waymarked gate to continue on towards a farm. When you get to it you are required to pass to the right of it through two gates to exit onto a lane.

Turn right on the lane (not immediately right through a waymarked gate into a field) which rises to a summit, just after which is a waymarked gate on the right. Ignore that to continue through a right hand bend and, on coming out of it, cross a stile on the right to follow the right edge of a field. The village of Tanworth-in-Arden is in view ahead. Cross a stile and footbridge bearing slightly left over the next field to find and cross another footbridge and stile on the far side. You are now faced with an upward sloping field and if you need any staying power at all on this walk it is here! Go up the field veering slightly right aiming to the right of the church to find hidden in the hedge on the right-hand boundary of the field a waymarked stile. If you find yourself at the back of a garden to a substantial residence you have not gone far enough right.

Cross the stile onto a path running between thorny hedgerows which emerges into the village and turn left back to the starting point.

## Shorter Walk

From the Winged Spur follow the long route down to point (3) where you go left along a field boundary. At the end cross a stile and go ahead across a short section of field to negotiate another stile (and footbridge) 100 yards ahead. Go forward now along the right edge of the next field, cross a further stile after 100 yards then keep to the right boundary of the adjacent field before going down some steps at the end to exit via a stile onto a lane.

Turn right then left after 20 yards (opposite Mockley Manor Nursing Home) over a stile and through a small copse to negotiate another stile into a field. The correct line now is straight ahead cutting off the corner to a stile you can see in the bottom left corner but you may feel more comfortable walking along the edge to get to this point. Heath Farm is on a rise to your left. Cross the stile and walk along the left boundary of the adjacent field, cross two further stiles in crossing boundaries before going through two gates onto a lane opposite The Coppice and turn right.

You need to walk along here for about half a mile so please take care as there is no footpath. You pass a water reservoir on your left then a little further on turn off left down a tarmac drive opposite The Warren. After 150 yards or so cross a stile on your right then another immediately on the left onto a grassy path alongside a fence running parallel with the drive leading towards a farm. All this looks fairly new and presumably intended to keep walkers off the driveway and divert them around the farm buildings ahead. As you approach the buildings you cross two stiles into a field and are then left wondering which is the correct way to go. The objective is the bottom right corner of the field some distance to the right of a farm cottage but I think the intention is that you should bear right after crossing the stiles to follow the fence line then turn left along the adjacent boundary down to the bottom right corner. When you get there cross the stile onto a grassy track between fence and hedge. The hedge soon ends and you go down to cross another stile. Shortly after this, and before reaching a gate, cross another stile on your right into a field and follow the left boundary. Ignore the kink in the boundary and continue to the bottom and go through a gate then another on your right into a field where you turn left. This is point (1) and you now follow the long route back into Ullenhall.

# 7

# Offchurch

## Fact*file*

**Maps:** Explorer 221; Landranger 151
**Distances:** Main walk 7.5 miles; shorter walk 3.25 or 5.5 miles
**Main Start:** Lay-by at Welsh Road Bridge over the Grand Union
Canal, 2.5 miles south-east of Offchurch (towards Southam),
which itself is about 3.5 miles east of Leamington Spa via a left turn
off the A 425. GR 385640
**Short Start:** The Stags Head at Offchurch, GR 360657 – see
above. .
**Terrain:** Pleasant countryside, an attractive village followed by a
stretch along the Grand Union Canal*. No climbs.

### The Pub:

**The Stags Head** in Offchurch. An attractive thatched village pub
dating back to the sixteenth century with olde-worlde interior,
beamed ceilings and a nooky fireplace, L-shaped bar and
restaurant. Serving Kronenburg 1664, Carling, Strongbow,
Guinness, Tetleys, Flowers, Batemans XXB and John Smiths. Bar
snacks and meals including home made dishes freshly cooked.
Beer garden. Open 12-2.30 and 6.30-10.30 Mon-Thurs, all day
Fri-Sun. Tel: 01926 425801.

From the lay-by walk away from the bridge towards Offchurch and, after a third of a mile, look for a crossing track and turn right. This is called Ridgeway Lane and although you stay on it for at least a mile and a half the surrounding views do vary considerably. The first section is enclosed by hedgerows and can get a little muddy in parts but, after a while, this changes and the track opens out with nice views to the right before you exit via a gate onto a lane.

Turn left on the lane and after a quarter of a mile go right at a junction along a slightly busier road which has no footpath, so please watch out for traffic. At the top of an incline after another quarter of a mile turn left along a track alongside Snowford House, back on Ridgeway Lane again. As you walk along here you get glimpses of the outskirts of Leamington and eventually arrive at a wide bridge crossing over the former Rugby to Leamington Spa railway line, which was closed to passengers in 1958. The view here over the deep gorge is quite spectacular.

Stay on the track on the other side of the bridge to exit onto the Fosse Way after a further third of a mile and turn left onto it. There is a grass verge of varying width but care is still required. As I hope you already know the Fosse Way is a Roman Road built in AD47 but the original stone is now several feet below the present surface. It was the western limit of the Roman General

Plautius's network of forts linking strategic points on the Rivers Trent, Avon and Severn. Regrettably there is no option but to walk along here for around half a mile to pass Fosse Farm and go down a dip to a point where the road is crossed by the former railway line (although this may not be immediately apparent) and a waymark post on the right. **1**

Take this right turn onto the path alongside a modern green clad barn and follow the long field edge through a crossing boundary and on to eventually exit at a lane after a distance of about three-quarters of a mile. You may notice a couple of stiles on your left along here which take you onto the line of the former railway track. Although the line will take you to the same end point I don't advise you to try this as the path is not maintained and gets very muddy and overgrown. Turn right on the lane and follow it down into Offchurch and The Stags Head. **2**

*OFFCHURCH. The tomb of the mighty King Offa of Mercia who lived between 750 and 790 is reputedly in St Gregory's church (which you can visit now or after refreshment) and the village itself is named after him. Offa's tomb is rumoured to be encased in the church and can be seen tucked away in the nave. Any trace of a palace he is thought to have built nearby on the banks of*

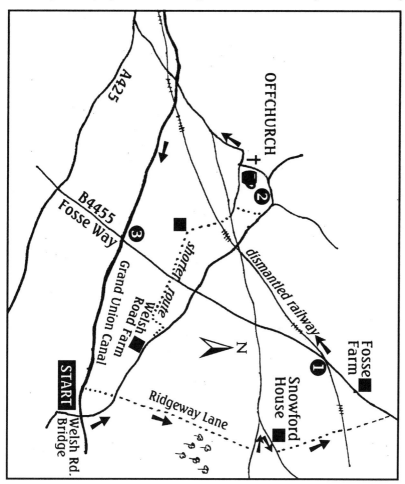

*the River Leam has been lost and the once powerful kingdom is now little more than a memory. Offchurch lies on the ancient Welsh Road, a drover's road which existed before the Romans came and built the Fosse Way. Stretching from Anglesey, through Shrewsbury and skirting round Coventry the Welsh Road travelled through Offchurch, past the Stag's Head public house and continued on its way to London. It was a thoroughfare for herdsmen to drive their sheep and cattle to market in London on a route where they could graze and be watered along the way. However, the village has more ancient roots as it was quoted as being 'a town of no small note in the Saxon times'. It also has the distinction of being owned in Edward the Confessor's time by Leofric, husband of the legendary Lady Godiva.*

Any urge to outstay your welcome should be firmly resisted and, upon gaining the exterior, turn left uphill towards Leamington. You shortly come to a junction where you turn right but, just after doing so, I strongly recommend you to have a look at the parish church of St. Gregory. It is a beautiful little church built in the twelfth century (see above) and the churchyard is part of the National Living Churchyards scheme designed to encourage a wide diversity of wildlife. There is more information inside but I think you will agree it is a most worthwhile project.

The lane continues with good views over towards Leamington. You reach a junction and bear right downhill on a footpath, which ends where the road goes over a brook. A few yards further on cross the road and cut left onto the towpath of The Grand Union Canal*. You immediately pass Radford Bottom Lock then go under the viaduct to the former railway. After a further three-quarters of a mile or so, having passed three further locks, you go under the Fosse Way road bridge. ❸

The locks between here and Napton are part of the 'Droughtbusters' project to overcome low water levels during recent dry summers. There is plenty of information about this on display boards. Keep going now for another mile past two further locks and under bridge No 31, which is in fact a continuation of Ridgeway Lane you were on earlier. I should also say that this entire section of canal is part of The Centenary Way*. At the next bridge, No. 30, after a further quarter of a mile, divert off left before it back to the starting point.

## Shorter Walk

Starting from The Stags Head, point (2), follow the long walk almost to the end of the text. You have walked for some distance along The Grand Union Canal* and having gone under the penultimate bridge referred to (No 31) turn off left up the embankment then turn right up 'Ridgeway Lane'. This track can get muddy in parts at times but, after about a quarter of a mile, you reach a junction with a road and turn left.

A distance of around a third of a mile will bring you to Welsh Road Farm and you continue past here on the broad grass verge until turning off left after another 150 yards at a waymark. Now bear right along the right edge of a field parallel with the road and, at the end, go 90 degrees left along the adjacent boundary. At the end of the field go right through a gap in the hedge across a drive and down a gravelled driveway alongside some cottages. You go through a gate onto a path alongside gardens, through a wicket gate to cross a small paddock and over a stile out into a field. Walk along the right boundary where good views open up to the left and the town of Leamington Spa looms ahead.

# Offchurch

You exit via a stile onto Fosse Way which you cross directly with care through a gap following the waymark directly across a field towards some barn conversions ahead. The path was well marked out at the time of my visit.

When you reach the properties continue on the wide grassy track to the right of them (*mmm*, not bad!) which ends in a field. Continue the line more or less across the field (again the path was marked) effectively cutting off the right corner and around the jutting in hedge and up the incline to the brow ahead. At the top you will find a bridge to cross over the former railway line and then continue on the path at the other side to a stile exiting onto a road. Cross and go down the lane opposite towards Offchurch but, after a little over 100 yards, cross a stile on your right and walk through a bit of vegetation to cross a footbridge out into a field. Cross the field more or less directly aiming to the right of a cottage on the far side to go over a stile onto a pathway running alongside it before turning left back to the pub.

# 8

# Claverdon and Wootton Wawen

## Fact*file*

**Maps:** Explorer 220; Landranger 139
**Distances:** Main walk 8.25 miles; shorter walk 5.75 miles
**Main start:** Anywhere convenient in Claverdon, a village located on the A4189 3 miles east of Henley-in-Arden and 5.5 miles north-west of Warwick. There is a lay-by opposite the Crown Inn and another just after the post office on the road to Shrewley. GR 195651
**Short start:** The Bulls Head at Wootton Wawen on the A3400 Stratford Road, 2.5 miles south of Henley-in-Arden. GR 152633
**Terrain:** A gentle walk over typical Warwickshire countryside taking in the fascinating village of Wootton Wawen and a section of the Stratford-upon-Avon Canal. One or two slight inclines but generally very easy going.

## The Pubs:

Another walk where you could drink yourself into oblivion and draw attention from the local constabulary. (*There is an adequate rail service to Wootton Wawen on the Birmingham/Stratford line!*). The featured pub is the Bulls Head at Wootton Wawen but I will refer to all four possibilities to present the full choice.
**The Crown, Claverdon.**
A convivial eighteenth century (though you wouldn't think it) hostelry with beamed ceilings and open fires. There is a lounge, bar and restaurant area and, like so many places these days, it is fairly heavily into food. Having said that it is the sort of place where you still feel comfortable just popping in for a drink. Serving Brew XI, Timothy Taylor, Caffreys, M & B, Worthington, Carling, Guinness, Grolsh and Strongbow. Beer Garden.
Open 11.30-2.30 and 5.30-11.00 Mon-Fri and all day weekends. Tel: 01926 842210
**The Navigation, Wootton Wawen**
Located on the bank of the Canal and next to one of the cast iron aqueducts along its length. The Navigation offers a wide range of drinks together with bar snacks and restaurant meals. Lockside beer garden and children's play area.
Open 11.30-2.30 and 6.30-9.30 7 days a week. Tel: 01564 792676
**The Bulls Head, Wootton Wawen**
What a fabulous place and one of the oldest buildings in the county. The external elevations are your original black and white and the roof pitches those hand hewn tiles with 'wavy' ridges. A photographers and painters ideal subject I would say. Internally, its

character impresses itself on your soul immediately and, as you would expect, is full of period features such as beams, stone flagged floors and open fires. Ales on offer include Banks's; Pedigree, Heineken, Guinness, a possibly a guest beer. Bar snacks and restaurant meals. Pleasant beer garden.
Open 12-3 and 6-11 Mon to Sat, Sun 12-10.30. Tel: 01564 792511
**The Crabmill, Preston Bagot**.
A superb looking place but a bit 'posh' for people in walking garb. Good selection of ales and top notch food.
Open 12-2 and 6.30-9.30 Mon-Sun but closed Sun evenings.
Tel: 01926 843342.

*CLAVERDON, meaning 'Claefer Dun' or Clover Hill in Old English, is a commuter village which successfully mixes the ancient and modern and boasts royal connections! In the church of St Michaels and All Angels there is a monument to Thomas Spencer, a distant relative of the late Princess Diana (Spencer), who died in 1629 at the age of 82. He built the Stone Manor which is a curious 3 storey structure which Pevsner considers to be a rare defensive tower-house. Another notable building is the seventeenth century forge with its unusual horseshoe shaped archway. There is yet another illustrious villager in the shape of Sir Francis Galton, a cousin of Charles Darwin, who developed identification by fingerprinting and whose early work Meterographica (1863) became the basis of modern weather charts. He is buried in the churchyard.*

With your back to the Crown turn right, crossing to the footpath opposite, and after about 50 yards bear left up some steps and over a stile into a meadow. Walk through the meadow just a little way in from the garden boundaries to your left then continue on the same line – there will probably be a marked route across as it appears to be a well used local path – down to a stile at the end. Cross and turn right onto a broad stony track which shortly swings left in front of The Lake House (do not be tempted at this point to continue ahead on a narrower path) and past some attractive cottages before going through, or more accurately round, a waymarked gate. Nice views open up now to your right over countryside around Henley-in-Arden.

You go through two more waymarked gates in close succession and come out along the edge of a field to the left of a fence. At the end is a choice of routes and we need to go ahead over a stile or through the wicket gate to the side of it , through a small thicket and across a stile into another field where we walk to the right of the boundary fence. Skirt round a group of trees to exit via a stile in the field corner onto a lane and turn right. Ignore a stile on your right after about 60 yards then shortly turn right at a junction to pass alongside some cottages. Also ignore a stile on your left just as you enter a more wooded section of the lane and continue past Kington Rise before shortly thereafter turning off left up a broad partially surfaced track known as Chestnut Rise. ❶

The raised area to your left, now developed, is called Tattle Bank and is of great interest to geologists. It comprises an area of sandy gravel forming a capping to underlying Keuper Marl red clay and was formed in the Ice Age 250,000 years ago when two great glaciers migrated here. At the top in front of Chestnut Rise Farm veer left along a bridleway, which can get churned up and muddy at times, to arrive at a stile by a gate. Cross onto a broad grassy swathe and shortly go through a gate to follow the right edge of a large field. At the end you go round a totally superfluous gate onto a broad track heading towards the extensive Cutlers Farm complex ahead. When you reach it bear round to the left then almost immediately turn right following a waymark on a gate post through the courtyard where you will see that much of the structure has been converted to offices. We are now on the Monarch's Way*.

Go through some gates at the end of the farm buildings and continue along the left edge of the following field. Pass through a gap in a crossing boundary and proceed forward on a rising course to the right of a tree line and, on reaching the top, bear right along the edge of Austy Wood. You shortly reach a gate taking you into the wood and, after a matter of only some 15 yards, keep right at a fork to enter a bridleway. Ignore a waymark left after a few yards and then fork right to continue on the bridleway, which can get churned up by

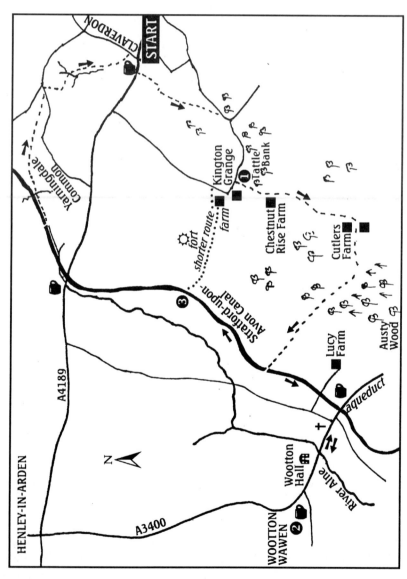

# Claverdon and Wootton Wawen

horses, until coming out of the wood when you stay ahead on the path as it continues between fields to reach a bridge over the Stratford-upon-Avon Canal*. The bridge is, or was, a split bridge allowing it to open to permit passage by larger vessels and is typical of many such bridges along the canal. Cross the bridge and turn left onto the towpath.

When you get to the marina and canal shop after about half a mile, cross the aquaduct and turn right down what can be a slippery path taking you under the aquaduct and out onto the A3400 with the Navigation Inn opposite, taking care how you cross the road. Now, if you can't wait any longer for a rest or particularly like waterside pubs then stop at The Navigation (see *Factfile*). However, if you can generate a little more energy by turning left on exiting onto the main road and walking along the footpath through the village of Wootton Wawen you will reach the Bulls Head which is a gorgeous black and white period building with a super ambience. **2** You will also pass a couple of interesting places along the way or on the return – see below.

*The Bull's Head, Wootton Wawen*

*The name Wootton Wawen comes from the Saxon meaning 'farm by the wood' and was founded in AD723 by Aethelric, although there is evidence of much earlier settlement. Hidden away behind the village shop, for example, is a huge arrangement of banks and ditches called 'Puck's Dyke' after an Iron Age spirit and there is an Iron Age fort visible to the right on the later canal section of the walk. There are many old houses in the village which have been carefully renovated in a mixture of styles and the seventeenth century Wootton Hall, now converted into flats and containing the village Post Office, was the home of Lady Fitzherbert who secretly married the Prince Regent in 1785. He later became George IV and she is said to haunt the property. In contrast, the church of St. Peter is absolutely awe inspiring and is the oldest in the county. It also has Saxon roots and is called 'The Saxon Sanctuary'. Religious and non-religious alike will appreciate the structure if only for its age, atmosphere and architectural style. There is an exhibition relating to its long history which is well worth looking at and you will learn much more about the history of the area than I am able to relate here.*

On a warm summer's day it may require some serious self-discipline to get motivated again. Return along the inward route but to get back onto the canal towpath I would recommend a little short cut by turning left up Pettiford Lane, a few yards past the garden furniture centre, and then right along the private road to Lucy Farm. When you reach the bridge turn left onto the towpath and continue past your inward point of access onto it for, perhaps, another two miles. Look for the Iron Age fort on a rise to your right referred to earlier. After about a mile those on the short route will depart at bridge 49. **❸**

Otherwise, at the next bridge you are required to leave the towpath in order to cross the road and continue along the other side of the Canal. Any of you still thirsty can turn left along the main road for 100 yards or so and you will find the most excellent Crab Mill pub and restaurant. At the next bridge you will again temporarily leave the towpath to cross a lane then pass by a lock-keeper's cottage built in 1810 with the barrel type roof often seen along the Stratford Canal (see also walk No. 4).

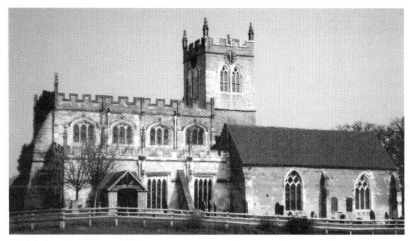

*St Peter's Church, Wootton Wawen*

At the next bridge by a lock, No 46, you leave the towpath for good by going directly ahead through a waymarked gate and along a field edge running parallel with the canal. At the end of the field bear left across two stiles then over a little footbridge into what looks to be a fairly boggy field. Now, what if I told you that the direction is diagonally across the field through the bog to the opposite corner? Well, it is, but I would suggest you skirt around to the right in order to err on the safe side! On reaching the corner go through a gap into the field on your right and follow the left edge of it on an upwards course and, at the top, cross a stile to continue the line forward in the next field, which in reality is a sports field. On the far side go through a gate onto a broad track in a wood to emerge onto part of Yarningale Common.

Turn left on the lane then immediately right down a stony driveway leading to Holly Cottage Kennels. When you get there you will find a choice of ways and should take the left option across a short section of grass and onto a path running to the rear of the garden to the kennels. Cross a stile and walk along the bottom edge of a field then cross two more stiles in successive boundaries. Now turn half right across the next field to a stile which is just about visible in the opposite boundary in a line of trees. There is also a footbridge to cross, after which you go straight ahead at a crossroads of tracks on a grassy path between tall hedgerows. After a further 120 yards or so look carefully for a waymarked footbridge on your right and cross it. This could easily be missed and if you come to a footbridge a short distance ahead on the original path you <u>have</u> missed it!

You very quickly cross another footbridge and stile into a field. Follow the left edge of it for a while and where the trees curve left continue the line ahead across the remaining section of field towards a tree line on the far side. Here cross a stile onto an enclosed path between hedgerows (careful of the holly!) to emerge onto a road in the village of Claverdon. Turn right back to start.

## Shorter Walk

Starting from Wootton Wawen, point (2) follow the long route out along the Stratford-upon-Avon Canal but only for a distance of around one and a half miles (from your entry onto the towpath) until reaching bridge No. 49 and point (3). Here leave the towpath, cross the bridge and go right over a stile into a field which you cross diagonally to reach the top right corner. Go through a gate here and walk across the centre of the next field passing just to the left of an electricity pole and on to a gate in the far boundary. You may be able to see an Iron Age fort up on the rise to your left. Once through this proceed on a farm track between fields and go through another gate with the farm buildings to the rear. You do not go up to the farm but turn left off the track at a waymark after only another 50 yards or so. Shortly cross a stile into a field which was at the time of my visit extremely muddy! Initially continue the line along a short section of hedge to a point about halfway between the stile and a corrugated farm building where there is another waymark directing you right across the field to exit via a stile onto a lane. Turn right and shortly pass Kington Grange then take the almost immediately following turning right along Chestnut Rise, which is point (1). Pick up the long route from here back to the start.

# 9

# Lower Shuckburgh and Napton-on-the-Hill

---

### Fact*file*

**Maps:** Explorer 222; Landranger 151
**Distances:** Main walk up to 8.25 miles; shorter walk 3.25 miles
**Main Start:** In the village of Lower Shuckburgh which is on the A425, roughly equidistant between Southam and Daventry. The best place to park is a lay-by adjacent to the canal bridge crossing just out of the village, beyond the church. GR 491628.
**Short Start:** The Folly Pie pub alongside the Oxford Canal at Napton BUT it is not the easiest place in the world to find. Napton-on-the-Hill itself is just off the A425 about three miles east of Southam. From the 'centre' by the Crown Inn and telephone box, follow High Street down and around into New Street to a point where the road sweeps left. Here turn off right by the sign to 'The Folly' along a narrow lane and over the canal bridge. GR 457607
**Terrain:** A wonderful mixture of peaceful canal and narrowboats, the picturesque Napton Hill and the Shuckburgh Estate. There are some truly magnificent views and, although there is some climbing to do on the second part, it is fairly gradual.

### The Pub:

What a find! What a gem! You won't find the **Folly Pie** on any OS sheet because it has only recently been re-opened as a pub (well, a few years now) after half a century. It is run by some enterprising individuals who combine the licensed trade with farming and much of the meat on the food menu is from their own stock. The Georgian building was clearly the original farmhouse. It is almost like stepping back in time a 100 years or so when you go inside – it is fantastic and I wish there were more places like it, a real English pub (with apologies to devotees of the theme pub). It is full of old artefacts and agricultural implements as well as having a huge open fireplace and just has that indefinable atmosphere which you get with somewhere a little special. Ales on offer include Folly Bitter and Godiva, both brewed by Warwickshire Brewery, Falstaff, Fosters, Harp, Guinness and Scrumpy Jack. Open during the week at lunchtimes during the summer (starting Easter) otherwise Sat and Sun lunchtimes only. Evenings from 6-11, 7-10.30 on Suns. Sometimes open all day on Sat/Sun at busy times. Bar snacks and 'folly fodder' meals. Large beer garden.
Tel: 01926 815185

---

# Lower Shuckburgh and Napton-on-the-Hill

From the parking spot cross the bridge, bear right down an embankment onto the towpath of The Oxford Canal*, then turn right again under the bridge (No.104). There now follows a long walk along the towpath which, with an optional extension, goes on for about four miles (i.e. half of the entire walk) but there is plenty too see. A warning though – the towpath is narrow and a little tricky to negotiate in parts, as well as being a little muddy, so please take care and you won't end up in the water!

You go under a number of bridges, including one with the enigmatic name of Nimrod (get it?), being the second time the canal passes under the A425 and for much of the way you have Napton in your sights. This is our destination in due course but we shall be approaching from the far side. You will reach a

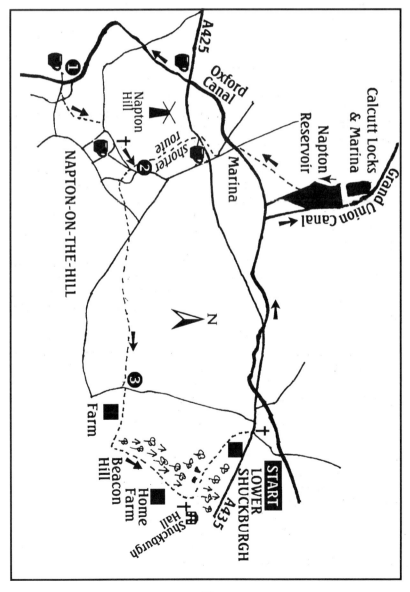

bridge where the Grand Union Canal* comes in from the right and here is where you need to decide whether to take the optional extension, which will involve about an additional three-quarters of a mile around Napton Reservoir and Calcutt Locks. It will also be necessary for you to cross a lock gate so if that is likely to worry you, skip the extension. In that case continue ahead over the bridge and pick up the text again after the next two paragraphs.

Otherwise, turn right under the bridge along the Grand Union. Napton Reservoir shortly appears on your left although obscured by trees; however, you will get a much better view shortly. You soon reach Calcutt Locks which is the start of a long drop westwards down to Warwick. There is an information board with further details. The Reservoir was built to overcome water problems in the canal system during dry periods. Now, this is where you are obliged to cross over the lock gate by the shop, so be careful! Next cross a bridge in front of the shop then bear left across another and walk along a section of pathway on the other side of the canal then out to walk along the top end of the reservoir.

Turn left at the far side to continue around the other side where a much better view of the water opens up as well as a wide expanse of surrounding countryside. The twitchers may find this an interesting place to stop awhile to see what's about. Before you get to the end of the reservoir divert right down an embankment and what can be a wet area of ground into a field which you cross to a stile on the other side. This is in fact a double fence stile and, once over it, cross the next field diagonally aiming pretty well in line with a windmill on top of Napton Hill. The windmill, incidentally, is restored and dates back to the sixteenth century – see below. Cross a footbridge between stiles and keep on the same line through the next field to the opposite corner where you cross a stile onto a lane by a bridge. Go immediately left through a gate and turn right under the bridge (No.109) to return to the main canal towpath adjacent to Napton Marina.

At the second road bridge (No.111) the Bridge Inn may present an irresistible diversion but please bear in mind that this is not the featured pub. This will be found about a mile further on at bridge No. 113 where you depart from the towpath to reach the Folly Pie Inn which is clearly visible to your right.

**❶**

I really wouldn't blame you if the urge to remain rooted to the spot became impossible to conquer, particularly as the more arduous part of the walk is yet to come. Perhaps when you eventually leave or get shown out by the landlord, walk over the bridge and after about 80 yards, look carefully for a stile hidden in the hedgerow on your left which you cross into a paddock and bear slightly right underneath an electricity line to negotiate a footbridge on the other side. Now cross a track which leads to a sewage works and go up a broad grassy track to a stile by a gate. Cross this, the next short section of field then another stile, or sort of stile, then cross the next square shaped and upward sloping field diagonally to the opposite corner where there is a stile giving access onto a lane.

Turn right on the lane and keep ahead at a crossroads to enter The Butts. Ignore next turning to the right going downhill but, after a few more yards, you have the option of turning left up a tarmac path to visit the church of St. Lawrence which crowns Napton Hill. It is well worth the effort and the views are tremendous. Those on the shorter route need not take this option as their way goes near the church from its vehicular access.

*The Folly Pie Inn*

*Napton-on-the-Hill, derived from the Anglo-Saxon 'cnaepp' a hill top and 'tun' a homestead or village. It is without doubt a dramatic and beautiful location. In the Middle Ages it was one of the largest villages in Warwickshire when it had about the same population as it does today. The last heir of the De Napton family married into the Shuckburghs in the fourteenth century and the two villages have been linked ever since. The hill rises to 452 ft. and has had a windmill on the top of it since 1543. Seven counties are said to be visible from the top on a clear day. Local legend tells us that the church was to have been built where the village green now is but the stones were mysteriously taken overnight to the top of the hill where the builders decided to erect the building. Some say it was the devil's work but the clergy at the time were hardly likely to have allowed building to proceed if they thought it was! More probably, it was thought that the new position was more dominant, which is certainly true. Much of the structure is thirteenth century and has some interesting features (leaflet available for those interested). Two grey gowned Elizabethan ladies are reputed to haunt it!*

Back on the lane, continue until arriving at a junction with a more major lane. Right on the left is a row of cottages with a footpath going up alongside the end   this is the short route back. **2**

Those on the long route should turn left into Vicarage Road but only for a few yards before going right in front of a property called 'The Granary'. You actually have to walk down a short driveway almost up to the access doors before crossing a stile on your left into a field. Walk along the line of a fence for a while and where this ends continue the same line to the bottom to cross stiles on each side of a track. You are now in a paddock and walk down the right side of it and climb over a fence into a larger paddock where you bear half right diagonally across to a stile in the far corner which takes you onto a lane. Before doing so there is a little brook to cross via a footbridge.

Turn left on the lane then immediately right over a stile into a field where you continue the line more or less diagonally across aiming about 50 yards to the right of a small building. You will find a stile on the far boundary with a fishing pool to your right where you cross another stile to walk by the left of the pool and around a short section of hedge to cross a driveway to a car park where you will observe that the said building is in fact a toilet block for fishermen. Could be handy if you are still recycling beer! You continue across a grassy area and cross another stile onto a lane where you turn right then immediately left over a stile and footbridge into a field.

In the field turn half right cutting off the bottom right corner and cross another stile about 100 yards ahead in the right boundary. Continue the line through the next field to a jutting in corner of an adjacent field under an ash tree, then follow the boundary on your right to the top of the field where you cross a further stile into the following field with a farmhouse in view ahead. Carry the line more or less ahead diagonally across to the top left corner where you cross yet another stile before bearing half right to cut off the bottom corner of another field to the next stile about 120 yards ahead. Cross this and a footbridge then again stay roughly on the same course aiming just to the left of the farmhouse to exit onto a lane. As you will no doubt have noticed you have been gradually climbing for some time now but the views are getting quite panoramic, particularly over to the left where you can see Rugby and even Coventry further to the left on a clear day. ❸

Turn left on the lane in front of Halls Barn Farm then almost immediately right by an information board relating to the Shuckburgh Estate, into an upward sloping field heading towards the right edge of a wood. Cross a stile and footbridge to continue the same line with some excellent views back towards Napton. At the top turn left over a stile by a gate into a field bordering the far side of the wood. Follow the tree line along (in a straight line – no need to follow all the ins and outs of the boundary!) over Beacon Hill, the top of which on your right is the highest point for some distance around at 730 ft. Continue ahead at crossing boundary through the next field parallel to wood then over a stile into the next and stay on the obvious course as the ground now starts to descend and a farmhouse comes into view ahead.

At the bottom of the field you go through a gate and join a track which soon peters out but you continue around the tree line to a stile by a large gate. Cross that into a parkland setting and now aim just to the right of a church ahead. When you get there you will see 'private' notices all over the place as you are now on the Shuckburgh Estate, so please respect these. The village of Upper Shuckburgh once here was deserted in mediaeval times. Shuckburgh Hall, a fine residence in a landscaped park, is not open to visitors. However, you can get a view of it and the adjacent deer park by turning right in front of the church for a short distance on the driveway running alongside the nearby farm (this is a public right of way). Squire Richard Shuckburgh, with his tenants, fought for Charles I at Edge Hill and was knighted on the battlefield. The church of St. Mary, with its many memorials to members of the Shuckburgh family, dates from the twelfth century though much altered in the late nineteenth century. Unfortunately this also is not open to visitors although you can walk around the outside. The way now is to bear left as if you were facing the church from the direction you approached it, along the sloping pasture around the base of a wood below it but dropping down the incline to a gate by a pool. There is a kissing gate alongside and once through that continue ahead on roughly the same line on a sloping field passing another pool on your left. You actually follow the line of some electricity poles to another kissing gate at the end where the beacon resides denoting its prominent position on the local landscape.

Cross the next field directly and the next stile 150 yards ahead aiming now in a direct line for the church at Lower Shuckburgh. After crossing a brook stay to the left of some cottages, go through a gate in a crossing boundary then turn left over another bridge before going diagonally over a field to the left corner. Exit via a stile which you cross into a lane running alongside St John the Baptist church – which is kept locked unfortunately. It looks fascinating with an unusual ornate hexagonal tower. It is Victorian and built in 1864. Notice the recently replaced village stocks funded by friends of the village. There is an information panel telling you more. Now just follow the lane for about 300 yards back to the start.

## Shorter Walk

Starting from the Folly Pie, point (1), work your way to point (2) and take the surfaced path upwards alongside the row of cottages. At the top you reach a junction with the lane leading to the church. Have a rest, then either visit the church or cross the lane directly on a path across a field and go through a metal kissing gate on the other side. Now continue forward across the bottom of a ridged field*, go through another kissing gate to stay ahead on a downward track. You can see the town of Southam due left and the largish village of Stockton on a half left bearing.

You shortly go through another kissing gate onto a narrow path, which is again surfaced, between trees which brings you out to the A425. Cross the main road carefully onto the footpath opposite and turn off left after about 30 yards over a waymarked stile. The Kings Head pub is just a short distance away if you can't resist a drink, or another drink, at this point. Cross the field diagonally right aiming to the left of a water pumping station to cross another stile on the far side followed by a bridge over a ditch. You now need to turn left onto a lane but not the one immediately on your left. Go ahead for a short distance to a junction and turn left here and follow the lane down to the canal bridge which you can see ahead. Cross the bridge and turn left onto the towpath of the Oxford Canal*. Completion of the walk simply entails a further one mile stretch of the canal back to the start. Before that a worthwhile diversion in the opposite direction will take you alongside Napton Marina and up to Napton Reservoir and even Calcutt Locks if you have the inclination – see long route.

# 10

# Coughton and Great Alne

---

## Fact*file*

**Maps:** Explorer 220 and 205; Landranger 150 and 151
**Distances:** Main walk 6.75 miles; shorter walk 4.25 miles
**Main Start:** From Coughton, which is on the A435 about five miles south-east of Redditch. If you intend to visit Coughton Court you can park on the National Trust car park there (the grounds open at 11am during the season – see further information below); otherwise there are several small parking spaces on the lane running alongside the Court – by the farm opposite or further along on either side of the ford. GR 083605
**Short Start:** The Mother Huff Cap in the village of Great Alne which is situated on the B4089 two miles north-east of Alcester. GR 114594
**Terrain:** Mainly easy paths across pretty countryside utilising parts of three National Trails. The walk starts (or finishes) with the splendid Coughton Court and also passes another, but considerably more modest National Trust property, Kinwarton Dovecote. No climbs of any note.

## The Pub:

**The Mother Huff Cap, Great Alne.** A most unusual place which claims to be a sixteenth century coaching Inn. Allegedly the name is unique and is explained in verse – see text. It has a small bar, which is clearly the original part of the pub with beamed ceilings and an inglenook fireplace, and there is a large veranda extension at the rear to accommodate the overflow. It has little in the way of modern trappings (with the exception of a coal effect fire in the inglenook and a fruit machine in the extension) and this helps to preserve its olde-worlde atmosphere. Serving Flowers, Tetley, Murphys, Carlsberg, Stella Artois and Strongbow. Bar snacks and meals. Open Mon-Sat 11.30-2.30 and 7-11; Sun 12-2 and 7-10.30. Tel: 01789 488312

---

*COUGHTON COURT: It's your choice whether to visit Coughton Court before or after the walk (or at all). If you do intend to visit I would suggest you do so at the end otherwise you may not experience the delights of the featured pub – there will be plenty of time providing you do not spend too much of it imbibing.*

*Home of the Throckmorton family, Coughton Court is one of the great Tudor houses of England. It has important associations with the Gunpowder Plot and saw much activity during the Civil War. The central gatehouse is impressive and so is the half-timbered courtyard. Inside are fine collections of furniture, porcelain and paintings. Opening times (2003) House and Gardens*

# Coughton and Great Alne

*15 Mar to 30 June daily except Mon/Tues, but open BH Mons and closed Good Friday. July and August daily except Mon, but open BH Mon, Oct Sats/Suns only. Times 11.30am-5pm. Entry charges £7.95, family £23.00; garden only £5.10. Tel: 01789 762435*

From the National Trust car park you need to walk along the driveway running in front of the Court and the two churches then turn left onto the adjoining lane. If parked on the lane itself start by walking in the direction away from the main road until reaching a ford and crossing it via the footbridge. You could in fact be parked close by the ford anyway or indeed beyond it, in which case you will need to walk back towards it but not cross it. I trust that is clear!

The ford in fact crosses the River Arrow and, I think you will agree, is a very attractive spot. Immediately after crossing divert off left along a broad waymarked track. Just to make things absolutely clear, if you are parked beyond the ford you will turn right just before reaching it. Elementary really. You soon go through a gate where there are signs confirming that you are on National Trust property and the Arden Way* and continue on the track going through another gate and looping right to the side of some apparently derelict farm buildings.

At the top of the short rise beyond (phew!) good views open up on both sides but particularly to the right over the Vale of Evesham towards the Cotswolds. Keep going on the waymarked track until you eventually exit onto a lane and turn right. Ignore a turning left and after about a third of a mile, just beyond some cottages, turn left along a waymarked track which is on the Heart of England Way*, the Monarchs Way* and the Arden Way with signs to Dinglewell Farm and Larkshill. ❶

You pass an isolated house and go through a gateway before bearing left after a further 100 yards across a stile on your left to follow a track across an upwards sloping field to another stile which you can see at the top. Once over this proceed in the next field with the boundary on your right and exit via a stile onto a lane. Turn right on the lane but after only 20 yards or so cross a waymarked stile on your right into a field where you move away from the left boundary to cross it diagonally heading towards the end of a line of trees coming in from the right. When you get there you will find a stile to cross into the adjacent field which you also cross diagonally in the direction of Dinglewell Farm.

Turn left in front of the farm boundary to walk across the long section of the same open field to reach the far boundary where you will find another stile. Again good views over towards the Cotswolds in the distance. This is in fact a fence stile and, having negotiated it, proceed in the next field adjacent to the left boundary and cross another stile at the bottom before going down a stepped embankment and continuing the downward momentum alongside the left boundary of a meadow. If you can see a water reservoir part way up the rise on your right you can be sure you are on the right track. You cross yet another stile at the bottom onto a lane and go ahead on this until reaching habitation on the outskirts of Great Alne. You go through an area of pretty cottages and, about 100 yards before the junction with the B4089, bear right on a waymarked path between gardens and paddocks.

Proceed through a kissing gate and continue forward (ignoring options right) into the churchyard of St. Mary Magdelene. At first glance it appears to have

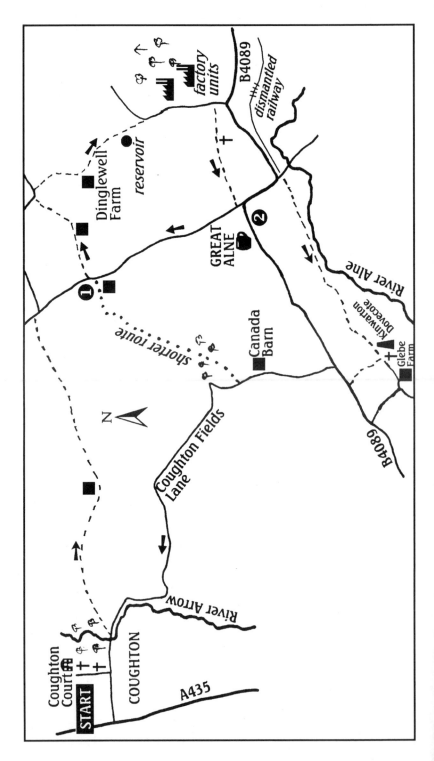

# Coughton and Great Alne

*Kinwarton Church*

been converted into a residence but this is only the church hall extension you can see and the little church itself is behind. Hopefully it will be open but to exit take the path opposite the entrance through a gate and turn left in a field. Go through into the next field and exit via a kissing gate to find the Mother Huff Cap directly opposite. **②**

GREAT ALNE, *bounded by the River Alne and known as 'Alwine' in Old English, meaning clear and bright. Flour was milled for centuries at a mill powered by the river until the 1980's. The Rockwell Standard Factory was located nearby and was one of many from Coventry which migrated to country areas during the last war to escape bombing. Even so, the village did not escape entirely. The factory still exists but has been broken up into units. Now, that curious pub name – the Mother Huff Cap. The meaning is supposed to be encapsulated in the following verse:*

> *'Twixt Michaelmas and Martinmas*
> *Old dame began to brew*
> *With half a pint of old malt*
> *And half a pint of new*
> *First twenty gallons of Huff my Cap*
> *Then twenty gallons worse than that*
> *Then twenty gallons as amber clear*
> *And then she brewed the servant's beer*

*Makes perfect sense doesn't it?*

# Warwickshire Walks to Wet Your Whistle

*Kinwarton Dovecote*

Love it or hate it, don't linger too long at Mother Huff Cap if you intend to visit Coughton Court at the end. You need to take the B4089 on leaving, towards Wootton Wawen and Little Alne. As the road swings left turn off right down Pelham Lane adjacent to the station house which has been converted to a residence. Immediately opposite is a kissing gate and you go through this onto a section of the former Alcester line of the Great Western Railway which has been opened up as a conservation walk. There is an information panel on the gate about this and the walk takes you on an attractive path through an avenue of trees with views over the Arden landscape and the River Alne. The path can get a little muddy in parts at times but stay with it for almost half a mile until going through another kissing gate and down the ensuing embankment. At the base turn left through a gate into a large open field.

In the field bear half right heading towards a curious circular structure on the far side. Once through a waymarked gate adjacent to an attractive pool continue towards the structure going through two more gates with a bridge between them. When you arrive at the building you may recognise it as a dovecote (Kinwarton) and this is also in the ownership of the National Trust. It was built in the fourteenth century and is still in use. In fact it has 500 nesting boxes and in medieval times the birds were used to supplement the meat supply of the Lord of the Manor.

*The opening times for 2003 are April-1 Oct 31 daily except Good Friday 9-6 or sunset if earlier. Cost £1. If closed a key and leaflet may be obtainable from*

*Glebe Farm. The dovecote and nearby church are all that is left of what has become one of the lost villages of Warwickshire. Do go and have a look at the little church which is absolutely charming. It originates from the thirteenth century although re-built in the mid nineteenth century – there is some beautiful stained glass and other artefacts of interest. Information board inside.*

Pass through a gate at the end of the dovecote field and immediately turn right through another gate into the adjoining field where you bear slightly right across it gradually, but not quite, closing with the top right corner. At the far end is a barely alive oak tree hidden behind which is a stile. Cross that to exit onto the B4089 and bear right before turning off left after 200 yards or so along Coughton Fields Lane. You now follow this for getting on for two miles all the way back to the start but don't despair - the lane is quiet and if you are with companions it will give you a good chance to catch up on some gossip!

## Shorter Walk

From the Mother Huff Cap point (2) follow the long walk almost to the end of the text to the point where you turn off the B4089 along Coughton Fields Lane. After about a third of a mile along the lane you pass Canada Barn on your right, a farm and extensive barn conversion complex, and about 150 yards beyond is a waymark on your left. Ignore that but after literally another 20 yards go right over a stile into a field. This you will note is a combination of three long distance paths – Heart of England Way*, Arden Way* and Monarch's Way* so following it should not present any major problems. Cross the field directly to a stile which you can see in front of a wood and cross that to proceed on a marked path through the trees to exit via a gap on the other side into a field.

Walk along the top edge of the field with some very nice views on the left over the Coughton area, but after a while look out for a waymark directing you right to continue on the same line but now of the other side of the boundary hedge. Now follow this almost to the end where you cross a footbridge and stile on the left before turning right alongside a house, cross another footbridge and a short section of field before going over another stile onto a lane. This is point (1) on the long route and you turn left then immediately right up a broad track to pick up the route from there back to the pub.

# 11

# Aston Cantlow and Wilmcote

---

### Fact*file*

**Maps:** Explorer 205 (mainly) and 220; Landranger 151
**Distances:** Main walk 8 miles; shorter walk 3.75 miles with alternatives.
**Main start:** The village of Aston Cantlow which is about six miles north-west of Stratford via the A3400, turning left at Pathlow to Wilmcote and on to Aston Cantlow. The village hall car park (opposite the Kings Head) is probably the best place to park. GR138601
**Short start:** The village of Wilmcote – see above. GR 164580
**Terrain:** Pretty villages, loads of history, woods, gently undulating country and super views. Sounds good and it is! A couple of short climbs but these are not particularly arduous.
**!** The path through Withycombe Wood can be extremely muddy so good footwear is essential.

### The Pubs:

There is an exceptionally fine pub in Aston Cantlow, **The Kings Head**, but the featured *en route* pubs are in Wilmcote and there is a choice of two.
**The Mary Arden Inn, Wilmcote** is an attractive three-storey early Georgian property, formerly a private house, which overlooks the Tudor farmstead which was Mary Arden's home (on the Stratford Tours). However, as mentioned in the text it does have a 'locals' bar serving Bombadier, 1664 Kronenburg, Fosters, John Smiths and Stella Artois. Food available all the time. Beer Garden.
Normal opening times. Tel: 01789 267030
**The Masons Arms, Wilmcote** is a traditional stone built village Inn with stone flagged floor, real fires and beamed ceiling to the bar. Extensions at the rear housing the restaurant which boasts an extensive menu. The name comes from the former quarry behind the building. Serving Black Sheep bitter, Hook Norton, Shepherd Neame, Boddingtons, Guinness, Stella Artois, Heineken, Strongbow and Blackthorne. Various bar games can be indulged in e.g. Jenga, Nine Mens Morris and Shove Ha'penny. Pleasant Beer Garden.
Open Mon-Sat 11-3 and 5.30-11 and Sun 12-4 and 7-10.30 but open all day in summer. Tel: 01789 297416

---

*ASTON CANTLOW has its derivation in the Norman, Canteloupe, which was the name of a baron who built a castle here in the early thirteenth century. His son, Thomas, became Chancellor of England in the reign of Henry III and was* canonised by the Pope. *The village has a very fine Guild Hall opposite The Kings Head thought to have been the home of the Guild of St Mary which provided priests for church services. It has now been converted into the village hall. The Church of St John the Baptist which is in need of repair and restoration at a cost of £300k is interesting and dates from the thirteenth century (last restoration in 1850). William Shakespeare's parents are reputed to have been married here and their first child baptised here in 1558. The church is littered with stories about the origin of 'The Green Man' an ancient personification of the power of the natural world. Common in places of worship throughout Warwickshire, the Green Man in this church is a carving on a bishop's seat made from old pew ends and is believed to have been the inspiration for many of the characterisations in Shakespeare's Midsummer Nights dream.*

From the village hall car park cross the road to walk along the left of the Kings Head towards the church (or turn right out of The Kings Head if you cannot resist a drink before you start). After you go through the gates into the churchyard fork left along the Arden Way* and at the end cross a stile onto a path bordering a pasture field. This shortly takes you over a footbridge to continue slightly left across the field to a gap in the top boundary, a little way in from the left corner. When you get there you will find a stile to cross which exits onto a lane.

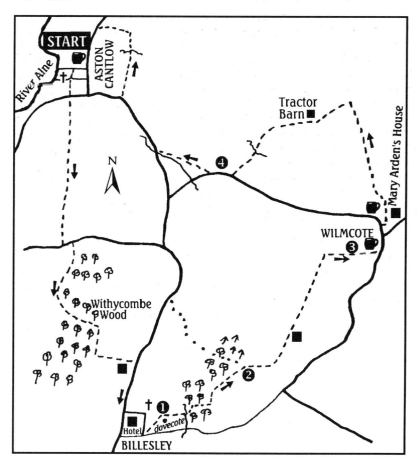

# Aston Cantlow and Wilmcote

Cross the lane directly to follow a waymarked broad farm track. Keep going along two long field edges for about three-quarters of a mile to exit via another stile onto another lane. This time turn left but, after 100 yards, bear right at waymark through a gate into a field. There are waymark posts in the field showing you the way across towards a wood ahead and, when you get there, turn right along the front edge of it. You go through a gate into Withycombe Wood, managed by English Nature, and stay on the main path, ignoring a waymark right, as it winds its attractive way through mainly deciduous woodland.

Eventually you come out and round the edge of the wood. You soon zigzag through a gap before continuing up to the next crossing boundary but do not go through the gap here; instead bear left along the right edge of the same field to some cottages in view where you exit onto a road and turn right.

After around a quarter of a mile you reach the isolated and curious hamlet of Billesley with the grand Billesley Manor Hotel the dominant feature. It was once owned by the Trussells who lived there for centuries. The last Trussell was hanged as a highwayman during the reign of Queen Elizabeth I. You can, if you wish, turn left here down past some very old farm buildings which look as though they could do with restoration (usual problem of who is going to pay, I suppose) to visit All Saints Church.

*The church is not without interest, being unused but in the care of The Redundant Churches Fund. Tradition has it that William Shakespeare married Anne Hathaway here. It was originally attached to a deserted medieval village of pre-Anglo-Saxon origin located in the adjoining field with the dovecote. As the information in the porch tells us, a combination of poor harvests, the Black Death and the eviction of peasants in favour of sheep farming brought about de-population of the village. By 1428 there were only four people living here. The original Manor House was replaced by the present building in the seventeenth century. There is more information and a key is available from the Hotel if you want to look inside, although you can see quite a lot just peering through the windows. The dovecote, which is still in use, is the only building from the medieval village that survives.*

Continue on the lane past the Hotel then turn left towards Wilmcote and, just past the hotel driveway, go left at a waymark and stile into a field heading for the dovecote in the middle of it. ❶

In the boundary on the far side of the dovecote you can see a waymarked stile. Cross and turn right in a field and, at the end, continue forward through a patch of rough and over a footbridge before turning left along the adjacent field edge. After about 100 yards you draw level with a stile in front of a wood on the right boundary and turn 90 degrees right across the field to reach it. Cross and proceed on a narrow path up through the trees and cross a further stile on gaining the top. Superb views open up here with Stratford off to the half right and the Cotswolds almost due right in the distance. Turn left along a broad track which soon swings right to follow a tree line downfield. At the bottom is a footbridge and stile and a choice of routes. ❷

Cross into a field and cut half right across it to the diagonally opposite corner and a gap in a line of hedge. The direction for people on the short route who have come through the gate is half left. When you get there cross a stile and turn right onto a broad farm track to the left of the hedge. You go over a crossing track with an equestrian centre over to the right to follow a course along the edge of a field towards Wilmcote. Just before exiting onto a residential road bear right at a waymark down a path between fences. Upon exit turn right then left to arrive at the Mary Arden Inn. You have a choice here – the Mary Arden Inn is, without doubt, very smart although there is a 'local's' bar approached from the front which has a stone flagged floor and where you should feel quite comfortable. Alternatively, if you go up the main street you will shortly arrive at the Mason's Arms which is a more traditional village Inn, although this too has a substantial restaurant attached. **❸**

*WILMCOTE owes its existence to quarrying in the nineteenth century and proximity to the newly built canal and railway system. The railway station still exists and has a regular service from Stratford. At that time over half the population worked at the quarries which produced a high quality floor stone known as 'blue lias'. Some of this material was used at the Palace of Westminster. In order to quench the quarrymen's thirst there were five public houses; now there are only two. If you take the road opposite the Mary Arden Inn you will find Mary Arden's House, which is open to the public. She was, as you all know, Shakespeare's mother and this is the place where he was born. Mary was the youngest of Robert Arden's eight daughters (how did he cope!!) and she inherited his property as he had no sons and she was the only unmarried daughter living at home when he died. There is also a falconry centre there. Entry will cost you £5.50 or £2.50 for children (2003). Open March–mid Oct Mon-Sat 9.30-5, Sun 10.30-5. Winter opening Mon-Sat 10-4, Sun 10.30-4.*

When you are all done find your way to a point half-way between the two establishments and turn off alongside a former church which now appears to have been converted to residential use. Cross a stile which takes you along a path to the rear of Mary Arden's House and then the Mason's Arms. Indeed,

*The Mary Arden Inn, Wilmcote*

you could have come out to this point across the beer garden to the latter but you weren't to know that. The way loops left over another stile followed quickly by another taking you into a paddock attached to a further riding establishment. Walk along the right boundary then cross two stiles to proceed along the left edge of a field.

Go through a gap in a crossing boundary and, after 300 yards or so – just where the boundary kinks – cross a stile on your left by a gate into the adjacent field and walk along the left boundary. Towards the end you will notice a tractor barn and should divert right to cross a stile and footbridge alongside it. Once over walk along the right edge of the next field and keep going until crossing another footbridge and stile in a crossing boundary. A continuation of the line in the next field will bring you to two further stiles which you cross to exit onto a road. Turn right along the road, taking care as there is no footpath. After some 250 yards you reach a waymark on your right where there is a choice of paths. ❹

If you are on any of the short routes please continue on the lane, otherwise take the left waymarked option into a field and follow the right boundary. The field narrows to a point and you continue into the next field but now to the right of the boundary. Where the boundary kinks go through a stile and turn right on another lane. In a third of a mile you come to a point where the lane swings sharp left towards Aston Cantlow and here turn off right (effectively continuing forward) across a waymarked stile into a field where you walk along the left edge.

Go through a gap in a crossing boundary and at the end of the next field cross a stile and footbridge to bear half right cutting off the bottom corner of the adjoining field to a waymark you can see on the right about 100 yards ahead, but here turn left (there is no left indication on the waymark post) on a track along the adjoining edge of the same field to exit onto a lane and turn left back to the start.

*Mary Arden's House*

# Aston Cantlow and Wilmcote

## Shorter Walk

Take the long route from point (3) out of Wilmcote through to point (4) and continue on the lane until you reach a junction where you turn left towards Stratford. After a quarter of a mile ignore a right turn and, after a further quarter-mile, at the brow of a hill there is a small pull-in. Just beyond it is a waymark directing you left into a field where you keep tight on the left boundary. As you proceed towards a dip in the ground you see a broad grassy track between hedgerows off to the right and it is this way you need to go. You are soon diverted right on what is effectively the same track but now with a hardcore base and you stay on this as it takes you up though a wood. At the end is a waymark post which indicates that you should go through a gate into a field where you immediately notice a footbridge and stiles and this is the point (2) referred to on the long walk. In fact if you were to bear right around the corner instead of going through the gate you would come to it from the long route direction. From here pick up the long route back to the pub.

There are at least two variations to the short route if you feel inclined to stretch your legs a little longer. Firstly, you could keep going on the lane down to Billesley, point (1) and pick up the long route from there back to Wilmcote. Another is to take the right turn which the above route says to ignore and follow that lane for about a third of a mile until you come to a waymarked gate on your left. From here you follow the long route from the second sentence of the second paragraph back to Wilmcote.

# 12

# Sherbourne and Charlecote

## Fact*file*

**Maps:** Explorer 221 & 205; Landranger 151

**Distances:** Main walk 8.75 miles; shorter walk 4.75 miles

**Main Start:** The village of Sherbourne which is easily accessed from Junction 15 of the M40 by taking either the A46 towards Stratford or the A429 towards Wellesbourne and turning left or right, depending on which option you have taken, after about a third of a mile. I have started the walk from the car park at All Saints Church but clearly you should seek an alternative on Sunday mornings or other times when the church is in use. There is plenty of street parking in the village. GR263612

**Short Start:** The Boars Head at Hampton Lucy which is located about two miles north-west of Wellesbourne. Take the B4086 from Wellesbourne and turn right after a mile up to Charlecote then turn left to Hampton Lucy. The village can, of course, be approached from various other directions. GR255571

**Terrain:** Easy going on mainly well used paths over pleasant countryside. Gradual gradients only but one difficult field boundary and footbridge to negotiate on the outward route.

## The Pub:

**The Boars Head:** a friendly little free house, built about 450 years ago, having beamed ceilings and cosy atmosphere. An information board tells us that it was attached to the living of Hampton Lucy and has little changed in the last 100 years. It is reputed that, in those days, one could only get through its doors on a Sunday with the permission of the Clergy! Serving Spitfire, Church End (brewed locally, see walk 3), Hook Norton, Theakstons XB, John Smith, Guinness, Strongbow, Carlsberg, Fosters and Kronenberg. Bar snacks and meals, beer garden. Open 11.30 – 3 and 6.30 – 11 Mon-Sat and 12 – 3 and 7 – 10.30 Suns. Tel: 01789 840533.

*The Church of All Saints is worth a visit although I was unable to do it justice as there were preparations for a funeral going on at the time. It has an octagonal ribbed spire rising to 150ft with eight carved figures of saints in niches – which is presumably from where the name derives. Its benefactor was Miss Louisa Ryland of Sherbourne Park who had the old church pulled down in 1864 and the present one erected at a cost of £20,000. There are a number of ornate internal features including the two-colour marble columns and font together with wood carvings of flora and fauna. Also, there is a memorial on the north wall to one of the dambusters.*

## Sherbourne and Charlecote

Walk back along the access drive to the church past the stables and out into the village, which would be your starting point if the church is in use. There are some excellent examples of Victorian estate workers cottages here and you go past these to turn left at a junction to continue along a pleasant lane for about a mile. Ignore any waymarks until you pass the elegant Court Farm House, after which the lane goes into a short dip. At the bottom of the dip bear right at a waymark along a driveway to Castle Farm and Castle Hill. ❶

You go past the farm and through an open gateway into a field where you turn left along the left boundary fence. On reaching the corner go straight

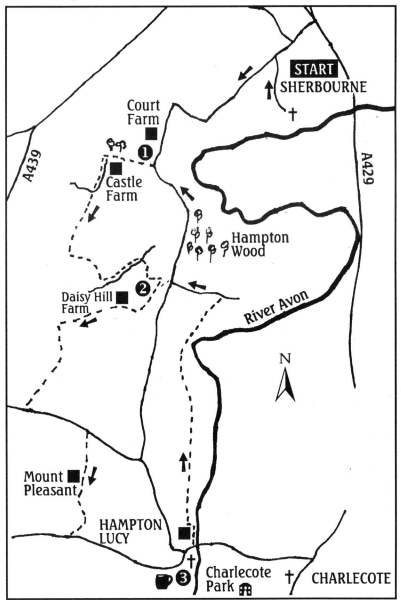

# Warwickshire Walks to Wet Your Whistle

ahead across a footbridge to effectively continue the line forward. The tall hedge on your left ends after about 80 yards and here proceed on a bearing slightly right to the far boundary where you will find a practically non-existent gate under a tree. It may of course have been taken away or replaced by now but, beware, the area around it can get muddy! Go though this then another gate into a field keeping tight on the right boundary and, at the top, you reach another gate.

Don't actually go through this gate but turn left along the adjacent boundary of the field and at the next corner go over a stile hidden in bushes to continue the same line in the following field. When you reach the end bear left to walk along the bottom edge of the same field adjacent to a brook. The way loops right at the end of the field where you are obliged to negotiate a rather precarious embankment to gain, then cross, a footbridge. *Please take care at this point.*

Once successfully across stay ahead to the right of the next field boundary with a large farmhouse in view over to the right, where we shall arrive shortly. As the ground becomes a little more steep look carefully for a stile in the hedge and cross into the adjoining field along the left edge. After some 150 yards you reach a waymark post in the hedge and here should divert sharp right (more than 90 degrees) across the field to a stile you can see between oak trees. **2**

Once over stay on line in the next field and, at the end, turn right in front of a gate along the top boundary of the same field. There are some good views from here. Just before you arrive at Daisy Hill Farm cross a stile on your left and turn right along the edge of a field before emerging to cross stiles on each side of the farm driveway. At the end of the ensuing short field cross a further stile into a large open field where you turn right to follow the boundary round. It soon veers left at which point you cross yet another stile and turn left to follow the boundary going away from the farm. From various points in this area you can obtain good views of the Cotswolds on a clear day and also the Obelisk in the Welcombe Hills to the north of Stratford (erected in memory of a former owner of the Welcombe Estate).

Cross a waymarked stile and stay on the same line in the next field. As the boundary swings left go with it and follow it round until you are led through an opening onto a path between trees to emerge and continue ahead in the same field! Eventually, you exit onto a lane and turn left. There is no footpath along here so please be careful as you need to walk for about a third of a mile before turning off right at a waymark down the driveway to Mount Pleasant. On reaching the property you should find a waymark on a post directing you to keep left alongside a fence. Where the fence kinks right continue ahead in a narrow pasture field to a point where the left boundary kinks and here cross a stile and turn right to continue ahead but now on the other side of the boundary. Exit the field via a stile onto a lane and turn left to follow it for half a mile or so into Hampton Lucy and the Boars Head. **3**

I hope that you have not been tempted to over-imbibe as your next stop is the Church of St. Peter ad Vincula, which is reached by turning right on exiting from the Boars Head. It is called 'The Cathedral in the country' and at the time of my visit was undergoing extensive refurbishment with the support of English Heritage. You really must have a look as the building is truly magnificent.

*Originally known as Bishops Hampton the Manor reverted to the Crown upon the execution of John Dudley, Duke of Northumberland in 1549. When*

## Sherbourne and Charlecote

*Mary Tudor became Queen she made it over to the Lucys of Charlecote, whence the village became Hampton Lucy. The suffix to St. Peter ad Vincula means 'in chains' (at the gates of Rome). There is another such dedication at Ratley on Edge Hill and when I wrote my previous book 'Walks Through History in the Heart of England' I ventured to say that it was 'rare'. Obviously not that rare! The church is built of Gloucestershire sandstone and its gradual erosion has prompted the need for urgent restoration. It is less old than you might think and was only erected in the 1820s in Victorian Gothic style, the former mediaeval church having been demolished following despoliation in the Civil War. Here are numerous features of architectural and historical interest but the overall impression is one of awe inspired by the towering octagonal pillars and high arched roof in the Early English style.*

*Hampton Lucy Church*

Continue on your way past the church and at a junction turn right to reach a bridge over the River Avon – one of the earliest examples of a cast iron bridge and purchased from Horsehay ironworks in Shropshire in 1829. You have a choice here. As you are no doubt aware Charlecote Park and its superb Elizabethan mansion is located close by and you can continue along this road turning right at the next junction to reach it. However, the distance is getting on for a mile each way (I have not included this in my distance calculation) and my inclination would be to finish the walk and visit Charlecote by car afterwards. You should have plenty of time to do this. If you do extend the walk or are obliged to do so for lack of transport please return to this point afterwards.

*Now in the care of The National Trust, Charlecote Park has been home to the Lucy family for over 700 years. The house is a magnificent Tudor mansion with imposing turrets and chimneys and is the epitome of this period in history, although the interior is largely modelled on early nineteenth century designs. Both Queen Elizabeth I and William Shakespeare visited frequently and it is said that the latter was caught poaching the estate deer! The deer park was landscaped by Capability Brown. There is no point in my going into more detail*

# Warwickshire Walks to Wet Your Whistle

*– go and see it! Open (2003) 8 March to 2 Nov daily except Wed & Thur. Times: House 12-5, grounds 11-6. Entrance (2003) £6.00, family £15. Grounds only £3. Tel: 01789 470277*

If you follow my recommendation do not cross the bridge but divert left before it down a public bridleway. After a short distance, go through a gateway leading to a residence then another in quick succession before turning left on a path between fences which winds around the rear of the property. You go through another gate and walk along the top edge of a field overlooking the river valley. You proceed along an avenue of spindly trees and exit through another gate into a field. Partway along this next field you divert through a further gate onto a narrow path adjacent to the field. The ground becomes a little uneven in parts and you exit via another gate to resume your walk along the field edge.

You come to a point where the path peters out into an open field. Do not be tempted to follow the right boundary but go directly ahead following a line of oak trees and, after the last oak, you come to a waymark post directing you right down the left edge of the field you were just walking above. Take a little care over direction here – after about 40 yards go left through a gap in the boundary into the adjacent field to walk along to the right of the tree line. At the end you reach an opening and a junction of ways; you need to turn left across the end of a field and around the base of a small hill to continue on a line veering to the right of a house in view to a gate in the far boundary. When you get there you will see that the gate is in fact on the other side of a lane and you do not need to use it. Instead turn left on the lane.

When you reach a junction turn right, unless you are following the short route, in which case you will turn left. Keep on the lane now past the nature reserve of Hampton Wood to continue on past point (1) and reverse your steps from here back to the start.

## Shorter Walk

From the Boar's Head in Hampton Lucy, point (3), follow the long route to the very last paragraph and the junction referred to. Turn left here but after a matter of only about 15 yards cross a stile on your right into a field and follow the left boundary. At the end of the field cross a stile on your left which is at point (2) then follow the long walk text back to point (3) – except of course that you ignore the first bit about staying on line after crossing the stile!

# 13

# Welford-on-Avon and Bidford-on-Avon

## Fact*file*

**Maps:** Explorer 205; Landranger 151

**Distances:** Main walk 8.75 miles; shorter walks 4.5 miles or 6.5 miles

**Main Start:** Welford-on-Avon, located about four miles south-west of Stratford off the B439 Evesham Road. Parking is available along the lane running up from the village green and the Shakespeare Inn, GR151518. Alternatively, you could start in Bidford just as easily, GR097518.

**Short Start:** Choose which short walk you wish to do. The starting points are either of the two featured pubs in Welford or Bidford respectively, or you could even start from The Cottage of Content in Barton.

**Terrain:** Easy going on well signed paths along the banks of the River Avon and across farmland.

## The Pubs:

If you really felt so inclined you could get well and truly legless on this walk as there are no less than three superb pubs along the route. I will give a little detail on each but I don't suggest that you visit them all otherwise your chances of actually finishing the walk will be greatly reduced.

**The Shakespeare Inn, Welford-on-Avon:** Although 'modernised' the pub has retained its olde-worlde atmosphere and offers Hook Norton, Bass, Greene King IPA, Tetley, Flowers, Guinness, Strongbow and various lagers. Food available. Pleasant beer garden. Open all day 11-11 except Sun when the hours are 12-10.30. Tel: 01789 750443

**The Cottage of Content, Barton:** A quaint brick and tile 'cottagey' property, as the name implies, serving Boddingtons, Tetley, Bass, Guinness, Heineken, Carlsberg. Restaurant and bar snacks with home cooked food; pleasant beer garden. Open Mon-Sat 11 – 2.30, Sun 12 – 3.00 and every evening from 6.00 except Sun at 7.00. Tel: 01789 772279

**The Frog and Bulrush, Bidford-on-Avon:** An idyllic setting on the banks of the river, particularly on a nice day when you can relax in the beer garden and watch the world go by – well that bit around the river bridge at Bidford anyway. Serving Greene King IPA and Abbot Ale, Bass, Worthington, Guinness, Stella Artois and Carling. Meals and snacks. If you are a devotee of bar games you might be able to play shove halfpenny, Evesham Quoits (a type of hoop-la) and Jenga – no idea what that is. Open weekdays 12-3 and 7-11, Sat and Sun all day. Tel: 01789 772369

# Warwickshire Walks to Wet Your Whistle

*Until 1931 Welford-on-Avon was in Gloucestershire and originally belonged to the Priory of Deerhurst in that County (see walk No. 24 in 'Walks Through History in The Heart of England'). Although rebuilt in the mid nineteenth century the church of St. Peter retains some traces of its Norman ancestry. The village itself is a slightly uncomfortable mixture of old and new properties but is not without a degree of charm. On the village green is a 65ft tall maypole, one of only five in the country. The original pole, known to have existed in the fourteenth century, was struck by lightning and replaced by a metal one which is repainted every ten years. Tales are still rife about 'Wicked Loddy', the notorious Lodvic Greville of Milcote Manor who was pressed to death with stones in 1589 for murder. The local children thought of him as a bogeyman to be lived in fear of. Perhaps they still do!*

If you can avoid starting without sampling the 'fayre' at the Inn (unless you are a late starter it will be closed anyway!), or even if you do, retreat to the road running through the village, turn left then immediately right down Barton Road. Walk through a pleasant residential area and after about a quarter of a mile take the waymarked path to your left leading between houses. Beyond the houses you continue ahead through an area of scrubby trees before crossing a stile and walking along the left edge of a narrow field, at the end of which you go through a gate and turn right to follow the hedge line in the adjacent field with Hunt Hall Farm in view over to your left. At the end of the field the way swings left along the adjoining boundary and you shortly go through a gap in the hedge to join a tarmac driveway heading towards the farm.

Stay on the track to the left of the farm buildings. It turns to gravel and twists right then left alongside barns and, at the first gate, follow the waymark through it passing by the remaining barns to another gate after about 60 yards. Once through cut half right across an open field slicing off the left corner – the line is not critical but you need to join the left boundary and follow it down to a waymarked gate in the bottom left corner. On a clear day nice views open up over the Cotswolds in the distance. Go through the gate and continue ahead on the same line in the next long field and at the end cross a stile and proceed on course in the next but, after about 80 yards, look carefully for a double stile with a dried up stream between (I hope it is still dried – there is no footbridge!) and after crossing the second, turn right towards farm buildings. Join and follow the fence line around the buildings and cross a stile on your right taking you onto a narrow lane.

Cross the lane more or less directly over another stile then proceed across the centre of a large field towards the settlement of Dorsington ahead. There is an arcing track in a dip which you can follow although this may not be quite so obvious if and when the field is planted. You reach and cross a footbridge on the far side into another field where you veer away slightly from the right boundary to a wicket gate in the far boundary. Once through cross a paddock diagonally left to find a stile providing an exit onto a quiet lane in front of The Old Rectory. Turn right through Dorsington with its beautiful mixture of thatched cottages and Georgian farmhouses. On the left you can see the remains of the moat around Moat House Farm. When you come to a junction, take the right turn towards Bidford and follow it on a twisty-turny course for perhaps half a mile until bearing off left at a waymark for the Heart of England Way* on the crown of a right bend. **❶**

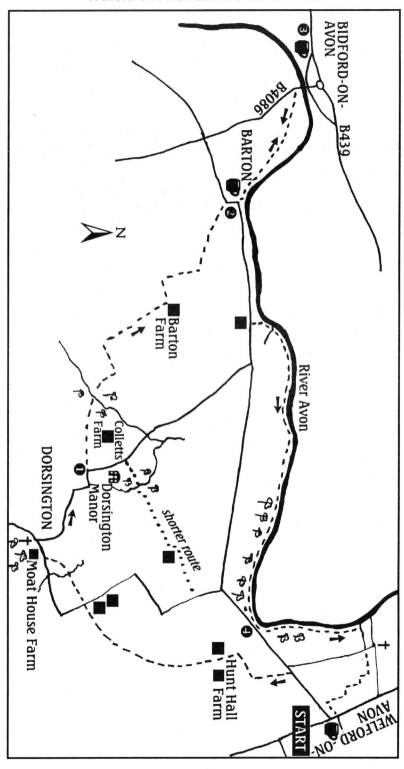

Follow the fence line on your right and after some 300 yards you are presented with a choice of routes. Take the right option through a gate to continue on the H of E Way where you next go through a squeeze stile in a crossing boundary then head towards a tree belt at the bottom of the next field. When you get there cross a stile on your left and follow the path round over a small stream and into the field beyond to continue adjacent to its left boundary. At the end bear left with a waymark into the adjoining field now with the boundary on your right. You go through a gap in a crossing boundary and, after a further 80 yards or so, turn 90 degrees right with a waymark into another field, again with the boundary on your right. There is another farm in view ahead and, when you get there, follow the path around the left perimeter onto the driveway where you turn left.

As you turn a right corner you can see the town of Bidford ahead, but you won't have to wait that long before a refreshment stop. The way leads you all the way down to the village of Barton where, upon reaching the road, turn right to arrive at The Cottage of Content. ❷

Choices, choices, choices! I will leave you to decide whether to patronise The Cottage of Content or continue on to the Frog and Bullrush in Bidford-on-Avon, or both! If a visit to the Frog and Bulrush in Bidford-on-Avon with its attractive riverside beer garden sounds tempting please continue with the next paragraph but bear in mind that the return route from there will involve re-tracing steps to Barton so, if the idea does not appeal, simply skip to the following paragraph.

Turn left along a surfaced access road to the side of the property and shortly cross a stile leading you onto the south bank of the River Avon. Walk along it for a while but before long you cross another stile which takes you down an embankment into a field, where you continue ahead to the left of the boundary. After going through a gap in a crossing boundary, cross a stile into an open field which you cut across diagonally half right heading for the outskirts of Bidford. Don't aim for the left corner of the field but a short distance in from it and in the crossing boundary you will find a stile. Cross this and the ensuing field on the same line aiming towards the river bridge. Go over a stile onto road and turn right over the ancient single track bridge (with care) then bear left to arrive at the Frog and Bulrush. ❸

*Bidford-on-Avon is one of the Shakespeare villages and is picturesquely set beside the River Avon which is crossed by a fine fifteenth century bridge. You can get a good view of it from the beer garden of the Frog and Bullrush. It has its roots in Saxon times, a fact which was brought vividly to life in 1921 with the discovery of an Anglo-Saxon burial ground. Excavation yielded a total of 214 internments, some of which were cremations with the ashes buried in beautifully designed urns. The town has the status of an ancient demesne, having been owned by Edward the Confessor and William I before passing to King John. This gave the villagers certain privileges, including exemption from further feudal services and some tax concessions. Opposite the church is the former Falcon Inn, now converted into flats, an impressive sixteenth century building where Shakespeare and his friends drank the Bidford ale and accepted a challenge from the locals to see who could drink the most. They lost and Shakespeare refused to return for another contest and pointed to each village in turn from a nearby hill and gasped 'No! I have had enough. I have drunk with*

# Welford-on-Avon and Bidford-on-Avon

*Piping Pebworth, Dancing Marston, Haunted Hillbro, Hungry Grafton, Didging Exhall, Papish Wicksford, Beggarly Broom and Drunken Bidford'.*

On a fine day the temptation to remain rooted to your seat in the beer garden may prove difficult to overcome. If you can, however, re-trace your steps to Barton and turn left on reaching the road by The Cottage of Content.

▶ You need to walk along here for about half a mile and should take care as there is no footpath for most of the way. You pass a solitary house on the right and go immediately left at a waymark along a track which shortly brings you to the River Avon again where you turn right along the bank. We follow this now for most of the way back to the start but please don't rush – this is a most attractive stretch of river with its reed beds and a quiet meandering course which makes all your stresses and strains just melt away.

You soon cross a footbridge and then a stile which is obscured behind an old boathouse. Another footbridge requires negotiating then a stile by a gate, then another stile before passing through a copse. You cross a further stile on the other side of the copse and continue onwards over the next which leads you into a slightly wilder section of path and yet another into a wood. You now walk along an elevated path above the river and, on emerging, arrive at a waymark with a choice of routes. ❹

If you are following short route 2, turn right here up the steps, otherwise continue ahead parallel with the river. Almost immediately cross a stile before walking through another wooded section and eventually the church tower of Welford looms up ahead. You are channelled along a path between hedge and a close boarded fence and shortly cross a stile alongside a modern barn which leads you onto a gravel driveway through a static home site with barn conversions on the left.

At the end turn right onto a tarmac access road and on reaching a road junction go straight across onto a gravel path signed 'churchyard extension'. You next go through a kissing gate alongside the extension onto a path which twists and turns until you are directed by a waymark left along a path which brings you to another kissing gate in front of a road in the village. Now simply turn left back to the start where you can, if you wish, enjoy more refreshment at the Shakespeare Inn.

## Shorter Walks

There are two alternatives, one starting from Welford and the other from Bidford. You could easily work out others starting from Barton or Dorsington.

### 1. From Welford and The Shakespeare Inn – 4.5 miles

Follow the long route to point (1) but do not turn off along the Heart of England Way. Instead carry on the lane passing the entrances to Collett's Farm and the south drive to Dorsington Manor and, after a further 50 yards, turn right along a public footpath which is the north drive to the Manor. You go along a stony track to the left of the property, cross a footbridge and a stile by a gate and follow the path as it curves around the rear of a small copse then straightens to continue along the adjoining field edge. Cross another stile and continue on line towards a farm ahead. Before you get there, you veer left through double gates then right following a fence line around the rear where you have a pleasant view over countryside to the west of Stratford. You cross another stile and a driveway to the property to follow a waymarked path to the left of a tennis court, beyond which you cross another stile into a field where you walk along the left boundary and an avenue of Hawthorne. Keep going until you exit onto a lane via a stile. Turn left now then right at a junction after 150 yards and stay on this lane for the remaining three-quarters of a mile or so back into Welford. If you wish to avoid walking the tarmac for the entire distance you could do so by cutting left down some steps after about a quarter of a mile onto the River Avon bank at point (4) and from here resuming the text from the main walk back to the start.

### 2. From Bidford and The Frog and Bulrush – 6.5 miles.

Turn right over the river bridge and cross the stile on your left into a field. Cross this half right and another in a crossing boundary to continue the same line diagonally across the next field aiming for the left corner. Here go through a gap in a crossing boundary and follow a path through another field to the right of its boundary. You arrive at and climb up an embankment before crossing a stile which takes you along a short section of the River Avon to another stile which you cross onto a surfaced access road and follow this for a very short distance to reach The Cottage of Content point (2). On leaving pick up the long route but from the point marked ▶ in the main text on page 73. Follow it through to point (4) where you turn off the river path up a flight of steps to reach a road. Turn right here then first left after about a quarter of a mile. After a further 150 yards cross a stile by a gate into a field and follow the boundary on your right down an avenue of Hawthorne. Cross a stile onto path alongside a tennis court, cross a driveway to the property and a stile opposite into a field.

Turn left in the field along boundary fence at the rear to pass through two gates on the left before turning right to follow the right boundary of another field. After going across two boundaries the gables of Dorsington Manor begin to impose themselves and you cross a stile by gates to walk along a track to the right of the property which brings you out on a lane. Turn left here past the entrance to the superb Collett's Farm and on the left hand bend in the lane some 200 yards or so further on you branch off right at point (1) on the long route where you pick up the text back to Bidford.

# 14

# Fenny Compton and Farnborough

## Fact*file*

**Maps:**Explorer 206; Landranger 151

**Distances:** Main walk 6.5 miles; shorter walk 3.75 miles

**Main Start:** Anywhere convenient in Fenny Compton, which can be reached via a turning west off the A423 between Banbury and Southam or, if travelling on the M40, come off at junction 12 to Gaydon then take minor roads south-east for about four miles following signs. There does not appear to be a public car park in the village but street parking is not difficult; I parked near to the War Memorial in Memorial Road. GR 417524

**Note:** This walk links up with the Fenny Compton to Northend walk (No 15) at point 3 in the text below. The seasoned longer distance walker could combine the two by picking up the Northend walk at this point. The total distance would be in the region of eleven miles.

**Short Start:** The Inn at Farnborough, which is also accessed off the A423 a little further to the south or by continuing through Fenny Compton towards Avon Dassett and taking a left turn for a further two miles. GR 435496.

**Terrain.** Wonderful rolling countryside on the edge of the Cotswolds including a section of the Oxford Canal*. A few gradients but nothing too taxing, apart perhaps from the hill after the pub if you are a little out of condition.

## The Pub:

**The Inn at Farnborough** is a most fascinating place, having been recently re-opened following a major re-fit, doing away with the old drinker's beer and fags type pub (shame!). It is a gorgeous up-market looking Cotswold stone building and first impressions are that this is not a walker's type hostelry, but look again – it has a stone flagged floor, huge fireplace, a comfortable but not plush interior and, yes, it is big on food, but also has a little corner for those who just want a drink. Altogether, a friendly, pleasant and well run establishment serving Hook Norton, Bass, IPA, Guinness, Stella Artois, Carlsberg and Scrumpy Jack. Beer Garden. Tel: 01295 690615

*FENNY COMPTON: On the lower slopes of the Burton Dassett Hills (see walk No. 15) and covering an extensive area. Quite a large village in fact with all modern conveniences. Many of the buildings are constructed of the warm brown ironstone from the old quarries in the Burton Hills which augments its attraction. Interestingly, Fenny Compton has the smallest water company in England, supplying about forty customers. The water is gravity fed from a spring in the Burton Hills and 'Fenny Water' as it is known locally is considered to be essential for making a perfect cup of tea.*

From wherever you are parked find your way into what is effectively the 'centre' of the village by the Merrie Lion Pub (yes, yes, you can have a drink before you set off if you must, if you're a late starter and the pub is open that is!) and go up Mill Lane opposite. Keep left at waymarked fork after about 100 yards then immediately right through double gates alongside a garage and shortly cross a stile into a field. Once in the field turn half left to cross it diagonally to negotiate another stile ahead in a crossing boundary. There is a footbridge here and, once over, stay with a field boundary on your right but before you reach the end cross a further stile and footbridge on the right to continue the same line but on the other side of the boundary.

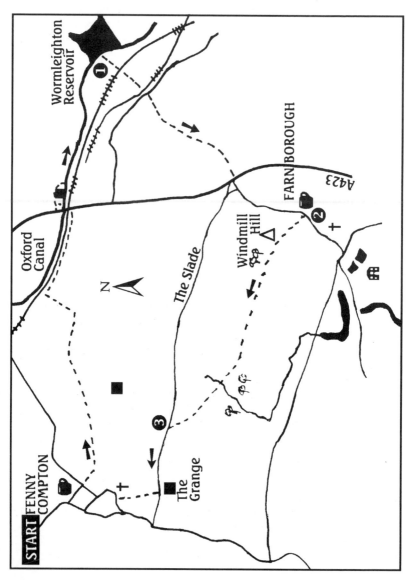

# Fenny Compton and Farnborough

After about 100 yards you reach a waymark post in the fence on the left directing you half right across the field cutting off the bottom left corner and you can see the next stile 200 yards or so ahead. This is another of those strip fields* commonly found in these parts which date back to medieval times when each peasant had his own little strip of ground to cultivate.

When you get there you will find that there is a double stile to cross and bear very slightly right up the slope and the next waymark soon appears in the form of a gate and footbridge and you emerge into a large open field. You need to cross the centre of this field slightly left and you may be lucky to find the way marked out with little posts with yellow tape fixed to them – full marks to the landowner/farmer; isn't it preferable to be shown the correct route across a field rather than wonder whether you are on the right line, possibly straying off it and needlessly trampling over crops? You are in fact heading towards a gap in the tree line and, when you get there, bear left along the edge of another large field to the bottom where you turn right along the adjacent edge.

You should now be walking parallel to a main rail line although it is hidden behind a vegetation screen in a dip. Almost at the far end go through a gate on your left onto the main A423 and turn left over the road bridge. There were some bridge reconstruction works in progress at the time of research which confused things a little but the best route is to bear right with the footpath diversion sign on the other side of the bridge through a metal gate onto a grassy path. The situation may have changed of course by the time this book is published!

The path takes you alongside some dilapidated corrugated buildings, after which bear right by what appears to be some old kilns and down onto the towpath of the Oxford Canal*, where you turn left onto it. Keep going to bridge No. 139, go under it and turn left at sign for *D'arcy Dalton Way* up steps and turn left over the bridge but, have a look to your right here over the quite attractively set Wormleighton Reservoir. ❶

*The D'arcy Dalton Way was created to mark the Oxford Fieldpath Society's Diamond Jubilee in 1986 to connect Oxfordshire's major long distance paths (we're right on the Oxon-Warwicks border here but just inside the latter) with the Wessex Downs and public transport links, and named after a notable defender of the county's path network.*

Go through a gate onto a grassy track and, at the end, cross the rail line with caution and continue forward under a bridge carrying a dismantled railway line and exit via a gate onto a lane. Cross directly through another gate and bear slightly right in a field cutting off the bottom corner and go through another gate in a crossing boundary and, once through, follow the fairly clear broad grassy track to some more gates ahead. Don't go through the gates you see at first but the others tucked away round the corner and, again, cross the next field on the clear track to the top corner. Here go through yet another gate with the outskirts of Farnborough in view and continue the line forward across the next field to pass through a gap to stay on the same course to the left of a boundary.

You join and continue ahead on a partially surfaced farm track which brings you out at a crossroads with the A423. Go straight across on a lane towards Farnborough and after about a third of a mile you come to The Inn at Farnborough. ❷

# Warwickshire Walks to Wet Your Whistle

*FARNBOROUGH: The village has lots of nice Cotswold stone buildings including the Kindergarten school and Reading Room. It was called 'Fernberge' in Old English meaning Little Hill of Ferns. If you have the time and inclination a visit to Farnborough Hall is an option whilst you are in the area. To get there follow the lane through the village and to gain the entrance follow the road round to the left then take a left turn. The hall itself was built of the same beautiful honey-coloured stone in the mid eighteenth century and is home to the Holbech family, although now owned by the National Trust.*

*Unlike many contemporary properties, Farnborough Hall and its landscaped gardens have experienced little alteration in the last 200 years and they remain today largely as William Holbech left them. From the grounds there are magnificent views across the Warwickshire plain towards Edgehill, Stratford and the Malvern Hills. It is open April to Sept on Weds and Sats 2-6pm. Admission £3.60, children £1.80. Tel: 01295 690002. One amusing little snippet I came across during my research was a marriage which took place in Farnborough on 20 May 1679 between Beata Penne and Job Knibb. Obviously, they became the PenneKnibbs!*

When you have summoned up the willpower to adopt an upright forward walking motion (other than to the bar for another drink or some other room in the establishment) cross the lane outside almost directly down a sort of waymarked alleyway between houses which soon turns into an enclosed grassy path leading up to a stile which you cross into a field. Cross this directly heading for the top right corner where there is a waymarked gate with a choice of routes. Take the option more or less straight ahead across the crown of a hill where there are super views all around on a clear day. The hill is called Windmill Hill, although the windmill has obviously long since gone, and you descend the other side of it towards the left side of a small copse, passing between that and some gorse bushes to reach a stile in the bottom boundary.

Cross the stile and walk along the left boundary of the adjoining field down to a footbridge which you cross into the next field. Where the boundary straightens after about 50 yards, veer half right to a stile in the right boundary, taking care to avoid a pool in the middle of the field. When you get there you will find another footbridge which you cross and turn left along the boundary of a large field. You are climbing here and, just as you reach the top of the rise, you come across a waymark post which directs you half right across the bottom corner of the field to a waymark post visible in the boundary under a tree. Go through into the next field which you need to cross slightly left to a waymark which sits in the middle of a short line of trees on the right boundary. Again the farmer had marked the way across with posts.

When you arrive you will find yet another footbridge to cross, after which go half left aiming well to the right of some farm buildings in view, still following the marker posts (which I hope are still there!). On the far side is a kissing gate and a footbridge which brings you out onto a narrow lane. This is the point at which this and walk 15 link up. **❸**

Turn left on the lane and as you descend past the farm the buildings of Fenny Compton come into view. You pass another farm called The Grange and, opposite the farmhouse, cut right through a waymarked gate which is shortly followed by another leading into a field. Go half left across the field heading directly for the church. You need to divert right a little to cross a footbridge over wet ground and exit via a gate in the corner. Go round the church and back to the start. Even better have a look at the church of St. Peter and St. Clare – there is an information board inside telling you something of the history.

## Shorter Walk

Starting from The Inn at Farnborough, point (2), follow the long route to point (3) and the exit onto a lane. Here turn right along the lane which is quiet and quite pleasant (called The Slade) and follow it through for about 1.25 miles until you are confronted by a gate across it. Once through that the lane loops right to another gate which brings you out onto a road where you turn right to walk the remaining third of a mile back into Farnborough.

# 15

# Fenny Compton and Northend

## Fact*file*

**Maps:** Explorer 206; Landranger 151
**Distances: Main walk** 6.25 miles; shorter walk 3.75 miles
**Main Start:** Anywhere convenient in Fenny Compton, which can be reached via a turning west off the A423 between Banbury and Southam or, if travelling on the M40, come off at junction 12 to Gaydon then take minor roads south-east for about four miles following signs. There does not appear to be a public car park in the village but street parking is not difficult; I parked near to the War Memorial in Memorial Road. GR 417524
**Note:** This walk links up with the Fenny Compton to Farnborough Walk (No 14) at point (I) in the text below. The seasoned longer distance walker could combine the two walks – the total distance would be in the region of eleven miles.
**Short Start:** The Red Lion at Northend, a village on the edge of Burton Dassett Country Park and situated two miles east of Fenny Compton and that much closer to M40 J12. GR 391525
**Terrain:** Undulating country with some magnificent views so pick a clear day if you can. A little climbing to do in the Burton Hills (before the pub!) but also some field walking. For those interested there is a wonderful redundant church to visit *en route*.

## The Pub:

**The Red Lion** at Northend is a pleasant if fairly traditional freehouse with a bar and dining room having a large open fireplace. Ales on offer include Brakespeares, Timothy Taylors Landlord, Brew XI, Tetleys, Guinness, Carling and Strongbow cider. Bar snacks and meals. Outside seating. Open weekdays 11.30-2.30 and 6-11, Sat 12-3 and 6-11, Sun 12-3 and 7-10.30. Closed on Mondays October to Easter. Tel: 01295 770308

*FENNY COMPTON: On the lower slopes of the Burton Dassett Hills and covering an extensive area. Quite a large village in fact with all modern conveniences. Many of the buildings are constructed of the warm brown ironstone from the old quarries in the Burton Hills which augments its attraction. Interestingly, Fenny Compton has the smallest water company in England, supplying about 40 customers. The water is gravity fed from a spring in the Burton Hills and 'Fenny Water' as it is known locally is considered to be essential for making a perfect cup of tea.*

Find your way up to the church of St. Peter and St. Clare, which is worth a look inside. There is an information board telling you something of the history. Go through the gate on the far side of the churchyard and turn immediately left through a waymarked gate and take the option half right around the edge of some marshy ground and over a footbridge to a gate in the right boundary. Go through, then after a few yards turn left on a lane opposite The Grange. After a short distance you pass another farm at the top of a rise and in a further 100 yards turn off right over a footbridge and through a kissing gate into a field. This is the point at which the two walks starting from Fenny Compton join up. ❶

There are two options here – go for the one more or less directly ahead across the field following the marker posts placed by the farmer to indicate the way across. Top marks to him/her. I hope they are still there. You are heading in the direction of Fenny Compton Hill and cross a stile and bear slightly left aiming for the next marker post you can see to the right of a tree about 250 yards ahead. Keep the line more or less the same in the next field to stay on the right of way, although in reality there is little point in doing other than walking alongside the right boundary. As you climb views start to open up to your left over towards Daventry and the telecom tower. You pass the end of a narrow spinney to be confronted by a large farm complex. Continue the line directly ahead across an open section of field to meet and continue along the mainly poplar tree boundary to part of the farm. You will pass an opening into the farmyard and reach a waymark post ahead which directs you across the next section of open field to a further marker indicating a continuation across another field heading towards the left side of a property in view. You will note that this is a permissive path to avoid walkers having to tramp through the middle of the farm, and I have no objection to that at all. When you reach a stile on the top boundary exit onto a lane.

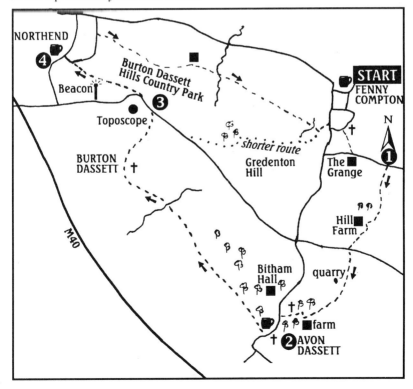

Cross the lane directly over another stile and walk downfield just keeping to the left of an old quarry to reach the bottom right corner where you cross another stile. This takes you onto an enclosed grassy path with a pool over to the right and you go through a gate into a field, which is upward sloping and where you walk adjacent to the right boundary. Towards the top go with a right angled kink in the boundary to cross a stile and turn right onto a driveway then veer immediately left on a grassy path alongside a tall conifer hedge. The path continues on a descent through a wooded area which brings you out onto a lane by a redundant church. This is not the redundant church referred to in the factfile although it looks equally interesting. Unfortunately it is kept locked although there is a key available for anyone who wants to look inside. Go past the church and continue into the village of Avon Dassett, where the eagle eyed imbibers amongst you will instantly spot The Avon pub. **2**

Turn right off the main street along a driveway running alongside The Avon (Park Close) and you shortly go through a gate informing you that you are on the Centenary Way*. Walk directly across a pasture field to the left of a group of oaks and cross a stile in the far boundary. Now bear half right on a worn path (effectively continuing the previous line) cutting off the right corner of the next field towards the right boundary. There are some very attractive mature trees around here which look absolutely stunning in autumn colours. You should also be able to see Bitham Hall over to the right. Bear left on reaching the said boundary and now simply follow the Centenary Way waymarks for a while through a number of crossing boundaries. There are excellent views over to your left to Edge Hill and across the site of the 1642 battle. You may also see the outline of The Malverns on a clear day.

You will come to a footbridge which you cross into a sloping field where you keep ahead aiming for a lone tree in a line on a brow – do not veer left up the slope but keep around the base of it. There may be some guideposts to show you the way. When you reach the opposite boundary there is a stile to cross into the next field where you follow the track heading towards a church to the right of a farm. Before getting to the end of the field cross a stile in a timber fence on the right then another shortly after, still heading for the church. Cross a fence cum stone stile into the churchyard.

*The ancient church of All Saints (thirteenth century) is now largely redundant although some services are still held there during the summer months. I would recommend a visit as it is quite simply magnificent. Not in the sense of size, though it is fairly large, or in ornateness, but in the magical atmosphere which exudes history from every piece of its structure. You feel as though you have stepped back in time for at least 100 years as it is little changed during this time; indeed much of what you can see is much, much older, including the fascinating medieval wall paintings. The air of antiquity is enhanced by some unusual architectural features, not the least of which is the sloping and stepped floor. The building is under renovation with the assistance of English Heritage – please support it if you can, not for religious reasons necessarily but because we should try to ensure that beautiful places such as this are not neglected in this age of cyberspace but preserved for posterity. Enough of my ramblings – there is a booklet telling the story of the church which you can purchase.*

Exit precincts through kissing gate and go ahead on a tarmac driveway, across a cattle grid and up to a signposted junction. **3**

# Fenny Compton and Northend

Keep ahead and admire the spectacular views, which will get even more spectacular if you climb up to the toposcope on your left. A 360 degree panorama unfolds through Edge Hill, Bredon Hill, the Malverns, Stratford, the Clees in Shropshire, Birmingham, Coventry, Daventry, Telecom Tower at Charwelton and many other places. The height above sea level is 630ft.

Keep forward where the road loops left to reach Beacon Hill. There are steps up to it and an information board at the bottom which tells you about the structure and a little about the Burton Dassett Country Park in general. It was the first of Warwickshire's Country Parks and extends to about 100 acres. If any of you thought it was originally an iron age fort or similar, you were wrong – the earthworks are the legacy of former quarrying activity. The beacon was built in the fourteenth century, but read all about it for yourselves. Interestingly, the size of the church indicated a much bigger population in days gone by and the answer to this can be found on the information board. Basically a combination of sheep enclosures in the sixteenth century and the Black Death. The name Burton Dassett is Saxon. In the *Domesday Book* it was written 'Decetone'. Dercett meant the 'abode of wild beasts' and 'ton' was an enclosed homestead. In this case the homestead was occupied by a man called Bur and his family. In

*The Beacon, Burton Dassett*

1908, quarrymen discovered a Saxon burial place on Pleasant Hill which contained 35 skeletons with injuries which are believed to have resulted from a battle in the sixth or seventh century.

Take a little care over direction now. From the small car park by the Beacon, go down through the valley below over a steep embankment to begin with – the route is not critical – and you will see a gate at the bottom at the end of a grassy path, still on the Centenary Way in fact. There is also a stile over to your right but ignore that. The village of Northend should be clearly in view. The gate takes you onto a path between hedgerows and you continue ahead along a driveway in front of some houses to emerge onto a lane. Go ahead here down Peartrees and follow the lane down to arrive at the Red Lion. ❹

When you have slaked your thirst and are ready for the off, retreat back past the earlier point of exit onto the back lane, which in fact is called Malthouse Lane and follow it left as it leads into Top Street. Continue almost to the end of the village before turning right up a broad waymarked track which is partially surfaced between houses. For the avoidance of any doubt there is a house on the right and a bungalow on the left. You soon go through a kissing gate into an upward sloping field and you follow the waymark direction on a trodden path to another kissing gate under a tree. Keep more or less the same line in the next (ridged) field* cutting off the left corner to join and continue along the left boundary.

At the end go through a further kissing gate then diagonally left across quite a large field aiming for the opposite corner where you cross a stile into the next field. You should now be on a broad track to the right of the boundary heading towards a corrugated farm building which you circumvent to continue on the track to the end of the field. Here you cross a footbridge and proceed directly ahead across the next, fairly large, field at the end of which is a gap (not waymarked). Go through into another open field and maintain course with the left boundary about 70 yards away and in the general direction of Fenny Compton church.

After a while you will see the yellow marker post on the far side of the field where you cross a footbridge in front of a stile into a paddock. Continue across the paddock to a metal gate on the far side to the left of a barn. Go through and turn left onto stony track which shortly loops right to meet a lane. Turn right then immediately left along Church Street back to the start.

## Shorter Walk

From the Red Lion point (4) follow the long walk to Fenny Compton and the end of the route. You don't actually have to go out into the village but, from the metal gate referred to, can turn right to cross the field alongside the green clad barn to a timber gate on the far side. However, you may just want to have a wander round – it is a pretty village and the church is interesting. There is also another pub, the Merrie Lion!

Anyway, go through that timber gate and turn right along a long field edge which takes you gradually upwards alongside Gredenton Hill towards Burton Old Covert. Views to the right towards Southam are good. At the top go through a waymarked gate then continue ahead initially in the direction of the Covert but the path then sweeps left in front of it by another of those ridged fields* and follows a course around the trees to reach another waymarked gate. Once through keep to the direction half left up a fairly steep incline with a fence line off to the left which juts in to a waymark post. This sends you off slightly to the right over the top of a steep rise but you can cheat by going around the edge on a gentler course. By whatever route, you need to gain the top right corner of the field to exit via a gate onto a lane and turn right.

Proceed on the lane and you will shortly enter the Burton Dassett Hills Country Park and reach a junction of lanes which is point (3) on the long route. You now effectively bear right to follow the long route back to Northend but, before doing so, I recommend you to divert left to visit the atmospheric semi-redundant thirteenth century church – see main text for a description.

*16*

# Hidcote and Quinton

## Fact*file*

**Maps:** Explorer 205; Landranger 151
**Distances:** Main walk 8.25 miles; shorter walk 6 miles
**Main start:** Both this and walk No. 17 start from the National Trust's Hidcote Manor Garden, which is just over the border in Gloucestershire, GR 175430. The best approach is from the Mickleton direction, which is on the B4632 about ten miles south-west of Stratford-upon-Avon and four miles north-east of Chipping Campden. There is a large open car park at Hidcote but I must emphasise that this is **only** for the use of people visiting the garden; therefore, if it is not your intention to visit I would suggest that you start from Mickleton or arrange to do the walk when the garden is closed – see details below.
**Short start:** The College Arms at Lower Quinton, four miles to the north of Mickleton just off the B4362. GR 183472.
**Terrain:** Pleasant undulating countryside and pretty north Cotswolds villages with some superb views. The trail takes in sections of three long distance paths and winds around the base of Meon Hill. There is a little climbing to do but, apart from the very last bit (apologies!), nothing too taxing. However, do not attempt unless reasonably fit.
If you are a lover of gardens you will be in paradise on this walk for there are two excellent ones to visit (long walk only). Please note the opening times and plan your walk accordingly to allow plenty of time to look around. Also, without wishing to overstate the obvious, you could plan to visit one of the gardens on this walk and the other on walk number 17.

### The Pubs:

There are two excellent pubs in Mickleton (The Kings Arms and The Butchers Arms – see text at point (1)) but the featured hostelry is **The College Arms, Lower Quinton.** This is a place of contrasts with the main part in stone and the remainder in brick, although that does not seem to matter. The wonderful, comfortable lounge with its beams and panelling contrasts with the more humble bar in front of which you can sit outside on a good day and look across the green towards the church. The building originates from the sixteenth century and has an interesting ownership history – see text for further information. Serving Batemans, Boddingtons, Hook Norton, Banks's, IPA, Flowers, Guinness and a variety of lagers. Restaurant and snack bar menu. Tel: 01789 720342

# Hidcote and Quinton

*Hidcote Manor Garden. Owned by the National Trust and one of the great gardens of England. It comprises a series of outdoor rooms, each with a different character, and is famous for its rare shrubs and trees. There are also many unusual plant species from all over the world together with some outstanding herbaceous borders. The varied style of the outdoor rooms peak at different times of the year making for an interesting visit at any time. Open April to Oct daily except Thur and Fri (open Good Friday); Times 10.30-6.00. Admission £5.90; family £14.50 Restaurant and tea bar. Tel: 01386 438333*

To start the walk retreat down the wooded access lane away from Hidcote to arrive at a junction with a lane. Directly opposite is the second of the two gardens, Kiftsgate Court.

*Opened to the public in 1981, Kiftsgate is set in an elevated position with superb views and contains many unusual plants and shrubs, including the largest rose in England – Rosafilipes Kiftsgate. It extends to five acres and comprises eight individual sections many of which are typical of the Arts and Crafts period. There is an elegant tearoom where lunches are also available. Open April-Sept, Weds, Thurs, Suns and BH Mon. Times 2-6pm, 12noon-6pm in June and July. Admission £4.30 Adult, £1 child. Tel: 01386 438777*

From the junction go straight ahead following a waymark under a tree through a gate into a downward sloping field adjacent to a wood. Go through

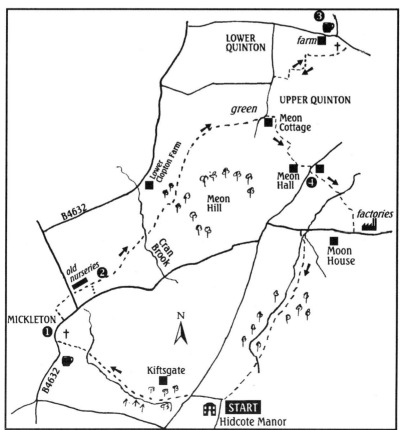

an opening in the trees, where there could be some mud about due to the presence of a stream, into another field and walk through the centre of it along an obvious track with pine woods to your left. The line is not critical and you will come to a crossing boundary where there is a waymarked gate just to the right of an oak tree. Once through continue the line more or less ahead slicing off part of the next field, aiming for the bottom corner. If the field is cropped you should be able to pick your way around the edge, if you prefer. The village of Mickleton is now clearly in view.

Go through another gate here, ignoring the stile on your left, and onto a well walked path along a field edge. At the end go through yet another gate and cut half right across a meadow heading towards the church spire. The approach funnels you into a short track between stone walls to the left of the graveyard to go through a gate waymarked Heart of England Way*. You keep ahead now on a roughly surfaced driveway taking you round to the left of the mellow Cotswold stone church of St. Lawrence. To my surprise this was open. It seemed bigger on the inside than it appeared from without and has some fine features, not the least of which is the stained glass behind the altar. Also there is a most unusual and colourful collection of kneelers made by local people. The driveway continues between some very attractive properties and deposits you in the main road running through Mickleton, just alongside the splendid Manor house. ❶

If you feel in need of refreshment already there is the King's Arms about 100 yards to the left or you can turn right, which is the way we are going anyway, and if you turn off left by the little fountain square you will find the Butchers Arms – a picturesque olde worlde establishment.

*It is not just the Butchers Arms which is picturesque, the whole scene along the main street of Mickleton is a wonderful mixture of Cotswold stone and timbered buildings. The Manor is home to the Graves family, one of the oldest in England. Sir Thomas Graves was a Vice Admiral and second in command to Nelson at Copenhagen. A more recent 'claim to fame' is that the village hosts the Pudding Club, founded in 1985 to prevent the demise of the traditional great British pudding. What a noble enterprise! It meets twice monthly at the Three Ways House Hotel where you can partake of a little spotted dick or the more unusual Lord Randall's Pudding, among many others.*

You go past the Three Ways House Hotel and come to a lane on the left called Back Lane. Right on the corner is a butcher's shop (although it was for sale at the time of my visit so it is possible that it will not remain as such) and you turn off left immediately alongside it on a grassy path which brings you out into a school playing field. Keep to the right hand edge of it and, at the end, cross a stile on your right into a field. Now walk across the field centre to a stile in the hedge line and in the break between two groups of houses behind. Once you have crossed this you will find yourself on the B4362 and you cross this directly onto a roughly surfaced driveway. Continue past some extensive and long abandoned greenhouses which were the former Meon Hill Nurseries. After the last greenhouse there is a track coming in from the right which is where the short walk joins us. ❷

Continue on the broad track through a large field heading in the direction of Meon Hill and stay with it as it joins a post and wire fence. At the end of the field you cross a footbridge over Gran Brook and negotiate a stile into Warwickshire to proceed half left across a field to the left of a clump of trees on the opposite boundary. If the field is ploughed up or cropped it is possible to walk partially around the edge although you are still obliged to cross an open section to achieve your objective.

When you get there cross a stile and turn half left across the bottom corner of a sloping field to another in the adjacent boundary. This takes you into the next field and you walk along the top edge of it whilst taking in the expansive views to your left over the Vale of Evesham. At the end cross a stile on your right and walk up the next field for a short distance before crossing a further stile on the left onto what can be a somewhat overgrown path through trees. You soon exit via another stile and cross an open field directly, passing by two large oak trees before negotiating two stiles in quick succession to stay on the same line in the next field. Lower Clopton Farm is visible below as is a blot of a scrap yard beyond. Thankfully, the Malverns are also in evidence in the far distance on a clear day.

You should now be walking to the right of the field boundary with the village of Lower Quinton in sight ahead, which is our next objective. There is another stile to cross just a little in from the field corner and, in the next field, you turn right to walk along the top boundary but, before getting to the end, you need to veer off half left down to a stile about 100 yards in from the right corner. You will find that this is, in fact, a double stile with a footbridge between and once over continue ahead across the bottom edge of the adjoining field to a further stile by a gate in the bottom opposite corner. Cross that and continue the line in the pasture field following, with the church spire directly ahead. Where the hedge line ends continue ahead but slightly to the right to a stile you can see in the far boundary. Cross onto a path between hedge and fence then go over a fence stile onto a lane, where you turn left although effectively carrying on in the same direction.

You shortly pass a waymark on your right next to a white painted brick and slate cottage (Meon Cottage) and you can shorten the walk by taking this and picking up the route again from the next paragraph. Sadly though you will miss out on a superb pub in which to take a break. Otherwise, make a note of this waymark and continue on and out into the lovely little settlement of Upper Quinton with its archetypal village green which you cross before turning right at a junction into Goose Lane. Now, please make a careful note of the section of route following as you will need to retrace your steps on the return leg. After a matter of about 100 yards turn off right down an access driveway to Lower Quinton Garage and after a similar further distance bear left into a field to the right of a tall bushy hedge. At the end of the field and hedge turn right along the adjacent boundary marked out with posts and tape which curves left before you are channelled over a stile and a fence stile on the right into an open field. You now turn left then immediately right across the field on a seemingly illogical route some 60 yards parallel with the left boundary. A farm is further to the left and, I am pleased to say, the farmer had marked the path across. Hopefully, this will always be the case. Follow the marked path through to a stile which is crossed into another field adjacent to the church. Keep the same line across it to a stile which provides an access to the churchyard. Go straight through and out onto a lane then bear left to find the College Arms. ❸

*Quinton, or 'Queans Town' in Saxon ('Quean' meaning woman. The village was in possession of the nuns of Polesworth until the Norman conquest.) was formerly part of the parish of Clifford Chambers and was transferred to*

# Warwickshire Walks to Wet Your Whistle

*Warwickshire in 1931. There are two villages, Upper and Lower Quinton, situated on the slopes of Meon Hill and each has its village green and a number of old houses. The parish church, though much altered, dates from Saxon times. The tomb of Sir William Clopton, who fought at Agincourt, is in the Chancel. The College Arms, Lower Quinton is sixteenth century and was originally owned by Henry VIII, purchased later by Magdelene College Oxford and remained in its ownership for 400 years. Because of the connection it is the only pub in England permitted legally to display the College Coat of Arms.*

Having walked a fair distance to get to this point, you may not feel like moving. At closing time or earlier, retrace your steps through the churchyard and across the fields to emerge onto the lane in Upper Quinton and walk over the Green again. You reach the waymark referred to in the last paragraph and

*The College Arms*

turn left alongside Meon Cottage and out onto a narrow path between hedge and fence to a stile which you cross before traversing a short field and turning right along the adjacent boundary of the same field again on a narrow path between hedge and fence. There is a bungalow now in view ahead. Continue through some scrub land to the left of the property and cross another stile into an undulating field. You need to cross this field diagonally to the opposite right corner.

Notice the strange pattern of undulations in the field. This is, in fact, an ancient strip field*, and you will see other examples in this vicinity. You may also have noticed that this path forms a section of two long distant paths, the Monarchs Way* and Centenary Way*.

Cross a stile into the next field and walk along the top edge, crossing a double stile and footbridge at the end to proceed upwards in the next field for about 50 yards before crossing another double stile and footbridge on your left. As you may have noticed by looking backwards, the views from up here are pretty good. In this next field the left boundary soon swings left but you continue the same line ahead across the remaining section of the field. The path was marked across at the time of my visit and, again, there are superb views from here. On the far side cross a stile with the delightful Meon Hall over to the right and walk over the ensuing paddock to emerge onto the access drive to the property via another stile. Turn left and wander down to meet a public lane. Turn right on the lane and after a few yards, just past a bungalow, cross a stile on your left into a field, unless you are doing the short walk, in which case you continue on the lane. ❹

Cross the field more or less diagonally towards a clump of trees on the bottom boundary with farm buildings in the background. Here you go through into the next field walking along the left boundary and, at the end, cut left through a gap then immediately right to cross a footbridge into another field.

# Hidcote and Quinton

Turn half right slicing off the bottom corner of the field to a waymark in the right boundary about 100 yards ahead. If the field is cropped you may be able to walk around the edge. Turn left now along the adjacent field edge and where the hedge veers 90 degrees right, follow it but gradually move away from it so that you finish in the top left corner of the field by the buildings referred to – which you will discover is not a farm at all but a small factory development. There is a stile to cross here onto a road where you turn right.

Please be careful along the road as there is no footpath. You pass Moon House on the left and after a further 300 yards or so, immediately after a belt of trees, turn off left across a wide verge and over a stile into a field. Look carefully on your left after some 15 yards for a footbridge, which has seen better days, hidden in the hedge. Cross it into the adjacent field which is effectively wedged between two brook courses and you keep to the right side edge following the course of the brook you have just crossed. Go over a stile and footbridge in a crossing boundary, then another to keep on an upward course alongside the brook. This is another strip field and you go through the end boundary into another field which you cross directly before going over yet another stile in front of a wood.

There is a little brook running past the stile which takes you onto a narrow path through the wood, which can get a little overgrown in summer. You emerge via a stile into a field to continue alongside the brook. You will see a waymark in front of another wood ahead where there is a low fence stile to cross. Again, the path through the wood can get a little overgrown and another fence stile soon brings you out into a large steeply sloping field.

Now, this is the killer bit and I would ask you to pay careful attention to the way! Go down the embankment in front of you then bear left up the valley. You will need to cross a brook via a footbridge and continue on looping slightly to the right and effectively staying in the valley until you reach the far tree lined boundary. Here there is a stile to cross if you still have the legs to do it and in the next field continue ahead along the bottom boundary. Where the hedge turns right carry on the same line across the open section to the bottom left corner to go through a gate back to the start.

## Shorter Walk

From the College Arms, point (3), turn left to the church and enter the churchyard. Cross it on the path and emerge via a stile into a field where you bear half right to a stile in the adjacent boundary. Cross that into a large field which you are now obliged to traverse on a seemingly illogical course about 60 yards out from the right boundary. The farmer had, thankfully, marked the path across but this assistance cannot be guaranteed to always be available. You reach the far boundary, cross a fence and turn left but after a matter of a few yards turn right over two stiles into the adjacent field.

This field has (or had) the way cordoned around with posts and tape and you turn left to follow the marked route along the boundary which curves right and then turns left on reaching the end of the opposite tree lined boundary. Follow the boundary on your right now down to an access lane to a garage and turn right to meet the lane running through Upper Quinton. Here turn left and walk across the delightful Village Green and, on the other side, look for a white painted brick and slate cottage on your left called Meon Cottage. You will find a waymark here and you turn along this and then pick up the long route in the paragraph after point (3) in the text.

Follow the long route through to point (4) and the exit onto a lane. Turn right and walk along the lane, ignoring the waymark on your left, and at a junction turn right again. Stay on this now towards Mickleton (please take care as there is no footpath although the road is not terribly busy) where you get some excellent views over the Vale of Evesham. When you reach the start of the built-up area turn off right up Nursery Close and take the one and only arm off it to the left. Directly ahead after about 60 yards at the far side of the turning circle, there is an alleyway. Walk along it for another 50 yards or so, bear right along a footpath taking you between houses and out to a junction with a broader track to the right of abandoned greenhouses. This is point (2) in the long text and you turn right and follow it through back to the College Arms.

# 17

# Hidcote and Ilmington

---

## Fact*file*

**Maps:** Explorer 205; Landranger 151
**Distances:** Main walk 6.5 miles; shorter walk 4.5 miles
**Main start:** Both this and walk No.16 start from the National Trust's Hidcote Manor Garden, which is just over the border in Gloucestershire, GR 175430. The best approach is from the Mickleton direction, which is on the B4632 about ten miles south-west of Stratford-upon-Avon and four miles north-east of Chipping Campden. There is a large open car park at Hidcote but I must emphasise that this is <u>only</u> for the use of people visiting the garden; therefore, if it is not your intention to visit I would suggest that you arrange to do the walk when the garden is closed – see details below.
**Short start:** One of the two pubs in the delightful village of Ilmington, four miles to the north-west of Shipston-on-Stour. GR 213436.
**Terrain:** Up hill and down dale over attractive north Cotswold countryside with some superb views. A little gentle climbing in parts and one fairly stiff one coming into Ilmington.
*If you are a lover of gardens you will be pleased to hear that another garden is located nearby at Kiftsgate – please see notes under the same heading in walk number 16*

### The Pubs:

There are two pubs in Ilmington and the contrast between them is very stark.
You can opt for the more sumptuous and comfortable (and pricey) **Howard Arms** where you can obtain a mouthwatering selection of home cooked fare chalked up on a huge board. The building itself is built in true Cotswold style and parts date from the early seventeenth century. It takes its name from the Howard family whose seat is at nearby Foxcote, which you will see from a distance on the walk. Don't worry about this not being a walker's pub - the bar has a stone floor and you should feel perfectly comfortable in here. Ales on offer include Marstons, Boddingtons, Flowers, John Smiths, Guinness, usually a guest beer and a selection of lagers.
Opening times, 11-2.30 and 6.30-11 with the usual Sunday variations. Tel: 01608 682226
Alternatively you could go for the village 'local' **The Red Lion** with its stone flagged floors and relatively spartan interior with prints of

---

old village scenes on the walls. Open fires in the winter and pub games to while away the longer nights. This is a Hook Norton pub so the choice of ale is limited. Food available.
Opening times are the same as the Howard Arms.
Tel: 01608 682366.

*Hidcote Manor Garden. Owned by the National Trust and one of the great gardens of England. It comprises a series of outdoor rooms, each with a different character, and is famous for its rare shrubs and trees. There are also many unusual plant species from all over the world together with some outstanding herbaceous borders. The varied style of the outdoor rooms peak at different times of the year making for an interesting visit at any time. Open April to October daily except Thur and Fri (open Good Friday); Times 10.30-6.00. Admission £5.90; family £14.50. Restaurant and tea bar. Tel: 01386 438333*

Go to the centre rear of the car park, through the double gates then turn immediately left through another gate into a field. Cross the field diagonally to the end of a line of trees coming in from the left and bear left to follow the adjacent boundary along the bottom of the remaining section of the field. Notice the strange pattern of undulations in the field. This is, in fact, an ancient strip field*, and you will see other examples in this vicinity.

At the end cross a stile and you are faced with a long undulating field in which you go more or less straight ahead following the valley. You are obliged to cross a stream then bear round to the left to continue more steeply down the valley until you near the wood at the bottom. Before you finally arrive there look for a line of gorse bushes along the embankment to the right and follow this line to shortly arrive at and cross a waymarked stile. This takes you onto a narrow path through a wooded area and it can get a little overgrown in summer. You emerge and go over another stile into a field which you cross directly on a course about 50 yards to the right of a tree lined brook. In a crossing boundary you will find a further stile which takes you into another wooded area where the path can also get overgrown at certain times.

You soon come out via a stile into the next field where you bear slightly left to go through a gap in some trees ahead and in the following field stay ahead on the line of the trees and brook to your left to reach a stile next to a cowshed. Cross this and stay with the tree line, go over a footbridge and stile into another field which narrows between two brook courses and, almost at the end, cross another footbridge hidden in the hedge on your left. Now turn right to a stile which takes you out onto a lane.

Turn right and follow the lane (care required, no footpath) past Moon House then a small factory site, ignore the subsequent turning left to Admington – where there is a blind bend to negotiate – and stay on the lane until you have gone about 40 yards beyond Larkstoke Cottage. Here there is a turn right down a narrower and rising country lane. About halfway up the incline bear left at a waymark onto a gravel driveway, and if you look backwards at this point you will obtain a superb view over the surrounding area for quite a distance – on a clear day that is. You will also note that you are on Centenary Way.* ❶

You very shortly arrive up against a gateway and are fed to the left through a wicket gate and down the right hand edge of a field. From here you can see that the gateway was the entrance to a very up-market stone built country house.

# Hidcote and Ilmington

You curve left at the bottom of the field along the adjacent boundary until you reach and cross a double stile on your right before continuing upwards alongside a post and wire boundary. There is a pool over to the left. Stay ahead at a waymark and, at the end, cross a stile and turn right along a path between hedge and fence. You cross a stile into another field and continue the line forward to the left of a mixed tree boundary. As you walk along here panoramic views open up through a 180 degree arc across a huge swathe of Warwickshire countryside. The village of Ilmington is in view ahead.

After about 80 yards, cross a stile on the right (ignoring one immediately to the right of that which provides access to a permissive path) and then turn half left (or right, depending on which way you look at it) in a field cutting off the top corner to pass through a group of willow trees before climbing up to an

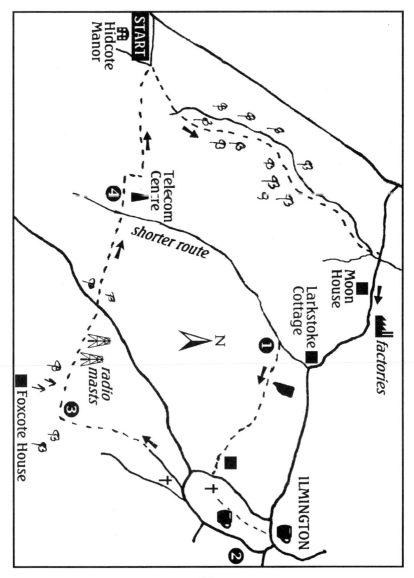

electricity pole where there is another stile. In fact there are two stiles and we want the second to stay on Centenary Way across a field aiming to the top left corner. There is a sheep track across and a waymark in the middle of the field to show you the way. This is quite a strenuous climb and at the next stile is another choice of routes. This time we need to take the left option going downhill on a broad grassy swathe. As soon as you reach a gravel driveway by a stone built cottage turn left through a waymarked gateway and walk across a small stable yard (look carefully for the waymark – you could easily walk past it as I did!) and out the other side along a path through some trees, down steps to emerge on a lane in Ilmington.

Turn right here and almost immediately left on a path to the right of the Church of St. Mary (unfortunately kept locked) and then left on a path behind it and right again. On emerging in a small square by a beautiful thatched cottage, bear left on a path bordering a brook. This pretty path runs along the rear of some stone built properties and broadens out to bring you to the Howard Arms. Now the choice is yours! As stated in the Factfile the pubs are as different as chalk and cheese and if you prefer the more 'locally' one turn right and after a couple of hundred yards or so you will arrive at the Red Lion. ❷

*The village of Ilmington is immensely charming and many visitors come here simply to take in the wonderful rustic atmosphere. With the decline of agriculture it has become more of a desirable commuter location but, even so, has retained its essential character to the point where some of the old traditions continue to be observed. The prime example is Morris Dancing – the village has the last surviving team in the county and they make regular appearances during the summer. The first Christmas broadcast by George V in 1934 was broadcast from Ilmington Manor and introduced by village shepherd, Walton Handy. E P Wilson the trainer of Grand National winners in 1884/5 lived here and trained horses on the downs. Keep your eyes about you though for more modern celebrities - the village, and particularly the Howard Arms, is a frequent haunt of actors from the Shakespeare Theatre at Stratford.*

When you can bear to tear yourself away go on past the Red Lion (or turn right on coming out of it) and keep on the road until turning left on a lane running along the rear of the war memorial. There is a small Catholic church here also. The lane develops into Grump Street and you pass some more lovely stone cottages before continuing ahead where the tarmac ends on a grassy path. Ignore a stile on the right and you come to another waymark with a choice of routes. We take the right option down an embankment and over a stile, then another shortly afterwards and turn left along a narrow field edge. The upward momentum continues and you cross another stile to stay on the same course in the next field. Again, a backward look will be rewarded with terrific views. Cross a further stile and, at the end of the next field, you reach the top of the climb and a crossroads of tracks. ❸

The splendid Foxcote House is down below and, although the way ahead will take you there, we need to bear right along the broad stony track. You continue along here for about two-thirds of a mile towards the radio masts ahead and with brilliant views on both sides. As you will appreciate you are walking along a ridge which is the highest point hereabouts, which is of course why the radio masts (Warwickshire Police Transmitter Station) are placed here. When you get to them you go through a gate and proceed downwards to meet a lane.

# Hidcote and Ilmington

Turn left on the lane then immediately right through a gate to follow the right boundary of a field to another gate at the top. Go through into a small wood then out along the right boundary of the long ensuing field. At the end go through a further gate onto a lane right on the border of Warwickshire and Worcestershire with Crown Castle International Telecommunications Centre opposite. **❹**

Cross the lane directly onto a broad path in front of the Centre and its satellite dishes with tremendous views ahead now over the Vale of Evesham towards the Malverns again. The track turns 90 degrees right then 90 degrees left on meeting a crossing track. You now descend steadily, go through a gate and you will see ahead of you Hidcote Manor and the starting point.

## Shorter Walk

Starting from Ilmington point (2) follow the route of the long walk through to point (4) and the lane in front of the telecommunications centre. Turn right on the lane and follow it for a little over a mile. Although this sounds like a lot of treading tarmac the lane is very quiet – hardly used in fact – very pleasant and with some magnificent views to enjoy. Ignore a waymark to the right and eventually you come to another, also on the right, leading you up a gravelled driveway. This is point (1) on the long route which you simply pick up and follow it back into Ilmington.

# 18

# Honington and Whatcote

---

### Fact*file*

**Maps:** Explorer 205; Landranger 151
**Distances:** Main walk 7.5 miles; shorter walk 3.25 miles
**Main start:** The hamlet of Honington which can be found just off the A3400, two miles north of Shipston-on-Stour. There is parking in the village but please be careful about it. I used a green verge down by the church which was well out of the way. GR 262427
**Short start:** The Royal Oak at Whatcote, about five miles north-east of Shipston- on-Stour and probably best approached by continuing through Honington from the A3400 and following the signs. Approach from the east along the A422 would be via a left turn into Oxhill and on to Whatcote. GR 299446.
**Terrain:** If you like visiting atmospheric old churches this is the walk for you! There are three of them and they are all superb. Apart from that the countryside is nice too – gently undulating with no severe gradients, although there are uphill sections around Idlicote. The villages are something special also.

### The Pub:

**The Royal Oak, Whatcote:** A twelfth century inn built as an alehouse to cater for workers building churches in the area. In the Civil War Cromwell used it as temporary quarters and the bread oven was removed to enable an observation slit to be made in the wall facing Edge Hill. It is said that Cromwell and some of his followers returned to the Royal Oak to slake their thirst and fill their bellies after the bloody battle. The quaint interior has an inglenook fireplace and beamed ceilings plus a genial host. Serving Hook Norton bitter and mild, guest beer, Carlsberg, Stowford Press Cider. Bar snacks and restaurant meals. Tel: 01295 680319. Opening times 12-3 (except Mons) 5.30-11, Suns 12-3 and 7-10.30

---

*HONINGTON – recorded in the Domesday Book as 'Hunitone' – the homestead where honey is made. The Manor was among the endowments of the Benedictine Priory of Coventry founded in 1043 by Earl Leofric, husband of Lady Godiva. After the Dissolution of the Monasteries it passed to the Gibbs family then in the mid seventeenth century to Sir Henry Parker who rebuilt both the Hall and the Church. The hamlet is a picture book of Cotswold stone and Tudor style cottages with huge manicured grassed areas to the frontages and it would not surprise you to learn that it was for some years rated as the best kept village in Warwickshire. The church is unusual for this part of the country, being more reminiscent of churches in London reconstructed after the Great*

*Fire. It is well worth a visit if you would like to see something just c̦*
*the ordinary. The thirteenth century tower survives as a separate struc̦*
*some of the old high box pews also remain. There are a number of o̦*
*monuments to the Parker family and their successors, the Townsends.*

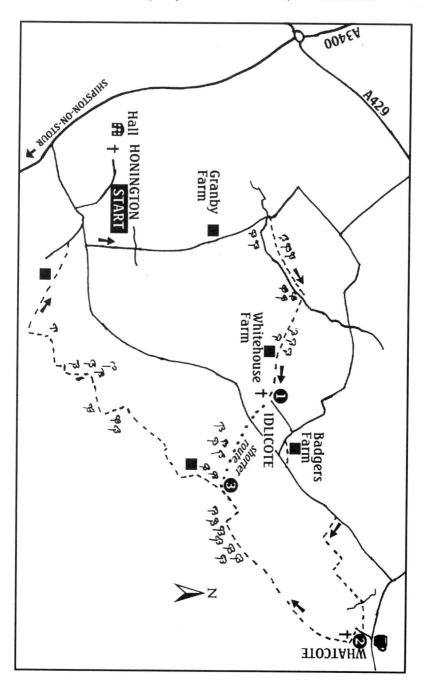

99

# Warwickshire Walks to Wet Your Whistle

Start by walking away from the church through the settlement and turn left at junction. Ignore the right turn to Barcheston but take the next left just after the chocolate box 'Rose Cottage' along a quiet lane signed Halford. You need to walk along here for a little over a mile but I don't think you will find that too much of a chore.

*Note on your left, just after leaving the built-up area, a ridged field\*. At the rear is the splendid Georgian Honington Hall – just the sort of place for me when I win the lottery!*

After a while you pass the neat complex of Granby Farm, whereafter the lane starts to descend and crosses a bridge over a stream before looping left. However, just after you cross the bridge, bear right through a gate onto a public bridleway with a dilapidated windmill to your left. Walk through the meadow keeping parallel with the tree and brook line on your right and at the end go through a waymarked gap to proceed along the edge of a wood. The way, which can get a little muddy, exits into a field where you continue a course along the bottom edge still with the tree and brook line to your right.

Go through a gate to stay on line in the next field and around a coppice before crossing a footbridge on your right, after which you follow a path winding through some trees to exit in a field. Here you turn left along the left side with the top edge of a tree line to arrive at Whitehouse Farm. Follow the waymark taking you ahead past the end of the barns then across the driveway into the opposite field. At the end of this field go through a gate and continue in the next on a rising course to the right of a post and wire fence with further farm buildings in view. At the top go through another gate but, before doing so, pause to take a look back over the surrounding countryside which, although not spectacular, has its own special beauty which typifies this part of the County. Proceed along a gravel driveway in front of various agricultural buildings and cottages in the secluded settlement of Idlicote. **❶**

*I found the hamlet totally charming but very secretive, almost as though it was not meant to be discovered. Indeed, it does have a few skeletons in the closet! In the mid sixteenth century a former incumbent of the Manor, Ludovic Greville was executed for murdering a servant and, towards the end of the same century, William Underhill was poisoned by his own son who was also reputed to have been executed, although there is some doubt about that. It is said that the village is haunted by the murdered man. A subsequent William Underhill was heavily fined in the reign of Charles II for wounding one, Devereux, with a pistol and on his refusal to pay his lands were confiscated in favour of Devereux. That was not the end of the affair for Underhill's men forced entry and ejected Devereux's men, killing one of them in the process. On the right is the very grand Idlicote House which also has quite a history and is now an hotel, and on the left a curious folly, the origins of which are a little obscure. A little further on you reach the church of St. James the Great. This tiny church dates from the twelfth century and contains box pews and the curious feature of a three-decker pulpit. The Chancel on the right contains memorials to the Keithley-Peach family, long connected with the hamlet and many of whom died in India while serving for the old East India Company.*

Just past the church on your right is a waymark on a gatepost, which is where the short routers exit into the village. Continue past this and along a straight driveway through what looks to be a former carriage entrance and

*The Idlicote Folly*

forward to a junction where you turn right. You immediately pass the gorgeous thatched Badgers Cottage and then look for a gate into the field on your left. Go through and cut across the field diagonally left to bottom left corner, cross a stile and exit through gate onto lane and turn left. You soon pass an agricultural complex on the right and, at the end of it, cross a stile or go through the gate then another gate after only 25 yards adjacent to the end of a barn into a small paddock. Cross this and a stile at the end with footbridge then turn right to walk along the right edge of an open field.

About halfway along the field you will find a waymark directing you left across the centre of it to go through a gap in the hedge on the opposite boundary. Should the field be cropped you may have to work your way around the edge to this point. Once through into the adjoining field turn right and get ready for an almost identical scenario, i.e. at waymark after 50 yards turn 90 degrees left across the field to the far side where you again go through a gap in the boundary. Continue forwards for a few yards to a waymark post (demolished at the time of my visit) which should direct you right across a bridge and across a field to the left of a line of electricity poles towards the village of Whatcote. You should be heading to the left of a relatively modern house and when you get to the far side you are channelled onto a narrow path between hedge and fence. Exit via a kissing gate into the village where you turn left to a junction then right to find the Royal Oak. ❷

*WHATCOTE, known as Quatercote in the Domesday Book stands at the crossing of two Roman roads. It has the dubious distinction of being one of the last places in England where the practice of 'rough music' was practised, where a couple who were found to be 'living in sin' were driven out by the inhabitants who gathered outside their house banging together metal objects to make a great noise and burning effigies of the offending couple. The village would be a very noisy place if the custom was still used today I'm sure! The church was almost destroyed by a German bomber in 1940 (thankfully, the only victims were sheep grazing nearby) and restoration work completed in 1947. Some of the earlier twelfth and thirteenth century windows and doorways survive. Whatcote also had a parish coffin which had loose sides so that no matter how poor the deceased person was, he/she could be taken for burial in a dignified manner but after the ceremony the sides and top were removed, leaving the body resting on the base.*

On throwing off any remaining traces of desire to stay put, turn right out of the pub then left into Church Lane. Go through the gate into the churchyard and keep left following the sign for Centenary Way* and out through a metal kissing gate. You immediately cross a stile and turn right in a field. At the bottom cross another stile into the next field where you turn right and follow the boundary round – do not go through an inviting gap on your right into the adjacent field. Stay on course over another couple of stiles towards a wood ahead. As you near the end of the field look for and cross a stile on your right then turn left to walk along the edge of the wood. You may be lucky enough to spot some deer in this area. I saw two in separate locations along this section of the route.

When you get to the end of this field bear right along the adjacent boundary away from the wood (there is a waymark on a dead tree stump). There are good views to the right now towards Edge Hill. At the top go through a gap on your left onto a roughly surfaced driveway across the centre of a large field. At the end you reach the corner of a wood and a waymark presenting you with a choice of routes. Main walkers carry on but if you are following the short walk you need to turn right at this point. ❸

Continue ahead then along the roughly surfaced track and keep left at a waymark just before an isolated house along a broad stony track. At the next waymark at the end of a paddock you go through a gap and turn right to walk along the right edge of a large field, or at least the bottom end of it. Go through another gap in a crossing boundary turning right to follow the next field edge but, after about 100 yards, zigzag through a wide gap to continue on line but now to the right of a field boundary. Just so you know you are in the right place there is another windmill in the middle of this field. You are following the Centenary Way waymarks all the way so, hopefully, should not take the wrong path.

Turn left through a gap in the bottom boundary to walk along the left edge of the next field. At the end go through yet another gap and turn right to continue past a small copse on your left to a wood, where you turn left to walk along the edge of it. Stay left at a fork (waymarked) around a pool after which the way curves right and you very soon reach another waymark which invites you to turn sharp left across the narrow section of field to stay on Centenary Way.

At the waymark on the far side turn right along the edge of the same field with some superb views over a vast swathe of surrounding countryside. You zigzag again through a gap and around the edge of a small copse before continuing downhill with the field boundary on your right. On reaching a junction with a farm track turn right onto it and proceed through two gates before arriving at a lane (open at the moment but it looks as though there are plans to put a gate across). Now turn right then left back into Honington.

## Shorter Walk

Starting from the Royal Oak in Whatcote, point (2), track the long route through to point (3). Turn right here down the adjacent field edge, go through a gap in a crossing boundary and continue the downward course in the next field. At the bottom divert slightly right to a stile exiting onto a lane which you cross directly through a metal gate onto a bridleway. What goes down has to go up and you now change tack to follow a rising way up the right side of a field to emerge through a small metal gate onto a narrow path and out onto a gravelled driveway. You soon go through some gates into the village of Idlicote where you turn right to rejoin the long route at point (1). However, before doing that I recommend you to turn left to look around the settlement, particularly the church of St. James. See details in long route text.

Now simply follow the directions back to the pub.

# 19

# Tysoe and Oxhill

## Fact*file*

**Maps:** Explorer 206; Landranger 151
**Distances:** Main walk 7.25 miles; shorter walk 5 miles
**Main start:** Anywhere convenient in Middle or Upper Tysoe in the south of the county about six miles north-east of Shipston-on-Stour. There are various places you can park; I used a small car park adjoining the now defunct fire station in Middle Tysoe. GR 339440
**Short start:** The Peacock Inn, Oxhill, a village two miles or so to the north-west of Tysoe and is readily accessible from the A422 Stratford-Banbury road which runs one mile to the north. GR 315457
**Terrain:** A little climbing after the start but otherwise fairly easy going over pretty countryside with some good views.

## The Pub:

**The Peacock Inn** has one large bar with beamed ceilings, an open fireplace and a convivial atmosphere plus a restaurant area. Serving Hook Norton, Ruddles, Bass, Worthington, John Smiths, Guinness, Carling, Heineken, Stongbow and Stella. Quite a selection I think you will agree. Bar snacks and restaurant meals. Beer garden. Tel: 01295 688060. Normal opening times, ie every lunchtime and evening.

From wherever you start you need to go out of the southern end of the village (Upper Tysoe) towards Brailes and Shipston-on-Stour. If you use the car park I suggest, this will require a left turn when you come out of it. Ignore all junctions off the main street and also a waymark left to Compton Wynyates, 150 yards after the road sweeps right along Shipston Road. Continue on through an S-bend, shortly after which you cross a stile on your left into a field. A windmill is clearly in view on the brow ahead and this is your immediate objective. Initially you aim slightly to the left of it across the field to gradually close with the left boundary to reach the top left corner where you proceed through a gap into an upward sloping field, now heading directly for the windmill. You wiggle left then right to reach the top.

There are superb views all around with Tysoe below and the southern part of Edge Hill beyond together with most of South Warwickshire down to the Cotswolds and across to the east over part of North Oxfordshire towards Banbury. If you have got a suitable map you should be able to pick out the various landmarks and villages. Go over a stile at the other side of the windmill and turn right across the top of an embankment with the stately Compton Wynyates, seat of the Marquis of Northampton, clearly in view below. You cross another stile and turn left on a fairly steep descent downfield after an initial flight of steps. At the base cross another stile and a bridge to enter a broad farm track which soon takes you over a further stile by a gate. The next stile will bring you onto a lane where the way is right. You can, if you wish, turn left for about a quarter of a mile to the entrance to Compton Wynyates but, to be frank, there is not a great deal to see – you get better views of it from along the path you have just walked. All the land is private (including the church it seems) and no longer open to the public. It has belonged to the Compton family in the direct male line since the early thirteenth century. The surrounding park is of Tudor origin and is reputedly on the site of a deserted village. ❶

After about half a mile turn right at a junction, immediately after which is the site of the medieval village of Chelmscote on your left although, again, there is not much to see except a few remaining earthworks. Shortly thereafter you

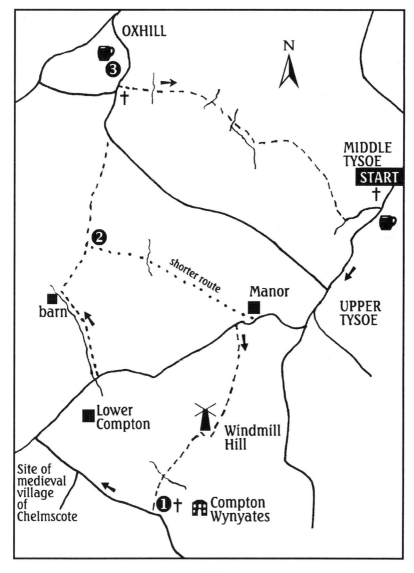

*The Tysoe Windmill*

sweep round a right hand bend and pass Lower Compton Farm on your right. Now look out for and take a waymarked bridleway on your left leading you along the edge of a field following the course of a brook.

At the end of the field, which is long and may be cropped up to the edge, go through a gate and continue a similar line in the next before going through another gate in a crossing boundary. Now, after a further 200 yards or so, you will draw level with a barn in the adjoining field on your left and, from this point, strike out 90 degrees right across the open field heading for the left end of a line of trees on the opposite boundary where you will reach a waymarked gate. At the time of my visit the field was not cropped but I imagine it could sometimes be so, in which case you may need to consider walking round the edge if the way is not marked across.

Go through the gate and another in short order into an open field which you cross diagonally to the opposite left corner. You need, first of all, to reference a lone oak then continue beyond that to the corner. Just beyond the oak there is a crossing right of way – the Centenary Way* – where the short walk comes in from the right. **❷**

At the said corner go through a gap into the next field and proceed alongside the left boundary. Where the hedgeline ends on the left continue the line more or less forward across the open section of field to a white gate you can probably spot on the other side. This you will find is at the entrance to Kirby Farm and you exit onto a lane and turn left. After a third of a mile you come to the church of St. Lawrence on the outskirts of Oxhill.

*Please visit the church if you can spare the time for, like many churches in this area, it is normally kept open. The dedication to St. Lawrence originates from a deacon of the early church who was martyred in AD258. The present building has a Norman doorway and many twelfth century parts. There are some elaborate Norman carvings around the south doorway and, internally, some fifteenth century oak benches and fine tower screen. In the churchyard is a most unusual headstone with the inscription 'Here lyeth Myrtella, Negro body slave to Mr. Thomas Beauchamp, Gent, of Nevis. Bapt. Oct ye 26th and buried ye Jan. 6th 1705.' Mr Beauchamp was a sugar planter which is the likely explanation of this un-English dedication. The name Oxhill itself, incidentally, has nothing to do with oxen on a hill but is derived from 'Ohtan Scylf', meaning Ohta's ledge of land.*

# Tysoe and Oxhill

Turn right at the junction or go via the church and out the other side in due course to arrive at the Peacock Inn. ❸

If you can avoid going under the influence it will assist in completing the last leg of the walk. Retreat back to the church and bear left at a waymark in front of the entrance gates across a private driveway and over a stile into a paddock area. Cross this diagonally to the opposite corner where you cross a stile by a beautiful thatched cottage and continue forward in a small meadow. At the end cross another stile and footbridge before walking along the right edge of the ensuing field. Stay on course until you reach a point where the hedge/fence kinks right and, just before it, cross a stile on your right and follow the corner of the adjacent field round for a few yards to turn left through a gap to continue on the same line as previously but on the other side of the boundary.

You cross a footbridge and farm track at the end of the field to stay on course in the next but, before the end of it, you need to go over another footbridge on your left to re-cross the brook then negotiate a stile to turn right and effectively stay on the same line in what transpires to be a very large meadow. After a further 60 yards there is another stile to cross which takes you through a thicket from which you soon emerge via a gate to continue ahead with the brook on your right. Cross a further stile in a corner and bear left in the next field and, at the end of it, go through a gate to continue forward to the right of a boundary.

Make for a gate on the far boundary a little way in from the left corner, now with the church spire of Tysoe in view. Proceed in the adjoining field about 20 yards parallel with the left boundary and after a further 200 yards, just as the boundary kinks right then left, there is a stile to cross on your left before turning right on a broad stony farm track. On reaching the farmyard, exit through a gate and turn left along a paved path in front of Orchard House then left along a lane which leads you to the church from whence you go along an alley directly opposite the entrance door to emerge into the main street back to wherever you started.

*Tysoe – the name has been suggested as meaning 'Tiw's hoh' which means a spur of land dedicated to the god Tiw, an anglo-Saxon god of war from whom Tuesday takes its name. There may be a connection here with the 'Red Horse of Tysoe', the name given to the figure of a horse cut into the hillside above the village. The turf had been cut away to expose the ruddy coloured soil in the shape of a galloping horse. It is no longer visible but legend connects Tiw with the binding of an evil beast, i.e. a story of good over evil and it may be that the original horse dates from the Saxon period, cut by them to commemorate a victory. The village was also formerly known as Temple Tysoe which suggests that it was once owned by the Knights Templars of Balsall. The parish church is rare in having kept its ancient dedication to the Assumption of the Blessed Virgin Mary. The Grade 1 listed building dates back to the eleventh century although, of course, most of it is later than that. It is a beautiful place, having been recently substantially renovated, and is full of interest. There is a useful guidebook available.*

## Shorter Walk

From The Peacock at Oxhill, point (3), follow the main walk route into Tysoe and walk right through the village to emerge on the other side at Upper Tysoe, as if you were starting the main walk. Pick up the text at the start then and pass the waymark left to Compton Wynyates. As you come out of the S-bend you have Tysoe Manor on your right and you follow the waymark through the entrance gates on the Centenary Way*. As the drive swings right continue forward along a grassy path through woodland which you soon exit via a gate into a field to continue the line directly cutting off the right corner. You meet the right boundary about two-thirds of the way along it and proceed through a gap at the end to continue on the same course in the next field.

About a third of the way along the edge you are directed right through a gap then turn left in the adjacent field although moving gradually away from the boundary towards what appear to be some railings on the far boundary. When you arrive there you will find that they are part of a footbridge which you cross into a large pasture field. Go over this, directly aiming towards a gap which you can just about see in the far boundary about 35 yards in from the left corner. Here there is a stile and plank footbridge to cross into rough pasture where you stay on the same line to arrive at a mid point just to the right of a lone oak. This is the pivotal point where the long route comes in from the left and continues up to the top left corner of the field. You need to turn right here to reach the same corner and pick up the long route at point (2) back into Oxhill.

More books by Roger Seedhouse

### WALKS TO WET YOUR WHISTLE

Eighteen walks covering some of the most beautiful countryside in Shropshire and along its Staffordshire borders, each providing an opportunity to visit a pub in which the walker will feel welcome and comfortable.

£6.95. ISBN 1 869922 41 7. 112 pages. 17 photographs. 18 maps.

### MORE WALKS TO WET YOUR WHISTLE

Following the author's highly successful first book he now presents a second collection of walks with a pub in Shropshire and along its Staffordshire borders.

£6.95. ISBN 1 869922 36 0. 112 pages. 24 photographs. 18 maps.

### WALKING WITH THE FAMOUS...AND THE INFAMOUS

A unique book of fifteen walks in Shropshire through areas associated with some of the county's most colourful historical characters. In an original and distinctive style the walks also relate the principal events of the characters' lives and are written as if through their own eyes.

£8.95. ISBN 1-869922-46-8. 128 pages. 15 maps. Illustrated with photos and drawings.

### WALKS THROUGH HISTORY IN THE HEART OF ENGLAND

The Heart of England is rich in history, both ancient and more modern, and the twenty-four walks in this book will offer the enquiring walker many intriguing glimpses of a bygone age – with iron-age forts, battle sites, medieval castles and even a second world war camp. All of them start at, or pass through, places of historical interest that will add greatly to your appreciation of a day out in beautiful walking country.

£8.95 ISBN 1-869922-41-7. 160 pages. 38 photos. 24 maps.

Available from booksellers or, if in difficulty, direct from the publishers. Please send your remittance, including the following amounts for postage and packing:
Order value up to £10.00 add £1.00; over £10.00 and up to £20.00 add £2.00; over £20.00 add £2.50.

**Meridian Books  40 Hadzor Road  Oldbury  West Midlands  B68 9LA**

*Please send for our complete catalogue.*

For more information visit the author's website: www.bestwalks.com